# THE BUDDHA'S TEACHINGS FOR BEGINNERS

# THE BUDDHA'S TEACHINGS for BEGINNERS

A Simple Guide to Connect
the Buddha's Lessons to Everyday Life

EMILY GRIFFITH BURKE

Illustration by KAILEY WHITMAN

ROCKRIDGE
PRESS

Interior and Cover Designer: Monica Cheng
Art Producer: Janice Ackerman
Editor: Jesse Aylen
Production Editor: Dylan Julian
Production Manager: Martin Worthington

Illustration © 2021 Kailey Whitman

Paperback ISBN: 978-1-6387-8109-7 | eBook ISBN: 978-1-6387-8242-1
R0

*To my teacher, Eve Decker,*
*and to the Southern Dharma Retreat Center community.*
*Thank you for continuously illuminating the path forward;*
*may we all be liberated from suffering.*

# CONTENTS

———�֍———

## PART III. THE NOBLE EIGHTFOLD PATH 53

## PART IV. OTHER BUDDHIST TEACHINGS 109

# INTRODUCTION

❋

Have you ever felt curious about what the Buddha teaches about human existence? Perhaps you've tried to meditate before or are just starting to build a practice. Have you contemplated what might be the source of suffering? Or maybe just wondered how you can use the Buddha's teachings, called *dharma*, to find more peace in your daily life?

If any of these apply, then this book is for you.

I wrote this book with the intention of introducing Buddhism, my spiritual tradition, to people who are curious about the dharma and seeking clear, simple explanations that connect the teachings to daily modern life in the Western world.

I am not an advanced retreat teacher, nor a highly realized meditator, but a committed, practicing, self-identified Buddhist human. I have a background in Tibetan Buddhism and have recently come to focus on Insight meditation. I teach dharma to kids and teens on the weekends, and guest teach with my local adult community, or *sangha*, a few times a year. I work full-time at a retreat center serving those seeking and sitting in immersive silent meditation retreats.

It also feels important to name that I share only from my specific identity location, that of a white, able-bodied, queer, privileged, lay Buddhist American woman. While I will aim to stay objective and informative in my sharing of the dharma, it is important to note that each of my identity aspects and the ways they intersect will inevitably inform my understanding. So, too, will the history of my relationship with the teachings.

I began attending weekly meditations and discussions in college, and for my first two years of practice, I engaged from a secular standpoint. I was a young, skeptical atheist and aspiring neuroscientist and not the least bit interested in spirituality. *And that was okay!* I learned early on that I was free to enjoy exploring the philosophy and psychology of the teachings without the spiritual aspects.

As you engage with this book, feel free to integrate only that which resonates with you, and set aside that which does not. The Buddha often uses the Pali phrase *Ehipassiko*, which translates to "come and see for yourself." I was drawn to Buddhism because it does not ask its practitioners to believe or practice anything on faith alone. The Buddha offers an invitation to engage with the dharma and see how it lands. If a teaching resonates, great! Practice, play with it, and see how it might integrate into your practice and daily life. If another teaching feels silly, unintuitive, or even harmful, set it aside; come back to it later and see if your relation to it changes. As you explore the teachings, empower yourself to listen to your own innate wisdom in terms of what feels true.

I hope by engaging with this book you are able to feel oriented to the Buddhist framework it offers. I wish that it may lead you to join a sangha, start a daily meditation practice, or simply continue reading dharma. Above all, may these teachings be of service to the liberation from suffering for you, me, and all living beings.

# HOW TO USE &
# UNDERSTAND THE BOOK

⎯⎯⎯⎯⎯⎯ ✻ ⎯⎯⎯⎯⎯⎯

About 2,500 years ago in Lumbini, Nepal, there lived a prince named Siddhartha Gautama who would go on to awaken to the true nature of reality and become the historical Buddha. Although the historical Buddha appeared in a male body, I would like to strongly emphasize that enlightenment itself is of a non-gendered nature.

It is said that when the Buddha awakened or reached enlightenment, he realized the true nature of all phenomena, a realization with the power to liberate oneself from suffering. This realization became the core of the Buddha's teachings. An extremely practical being, Buddha focused his teachings on personal contemplation of inner experience to illuminate the path from suffering to liberation. Considering that, the core teachings are quite simple and practical, and often appear in the form of numbered lists.

The three main teachings offered in this book are the Three Marks of Existence, the Four Noble Truths, and the Noble Eightfold Path. The Three Marks of Existence describe the Buddha's realizations about the nature of our lived experiences, like human suffering, or *dukkha*. The Four Noble Truths expand on this by addressing the nature of dukkha and where it comes from. Finally, the last of the Four Noble Truths points to the Noble Eightfold Path as the way to liberation from dukkha.

I recommend first exploring the Three Marks of Existence and the Four Noble Truths before diving into the Noble Eightfold Path. As you contemplate the first two teachings, read slowly, pausing to experience the words in your body and Heartspace. By examining the first two core teachings in this way, you will build a framework of understanding and deep knowing that may uncover your natural curiosity and motivation to pursue the Path. That said, I will always support practitioners following their own intuition and sense of truth. It is said that the wisdom of these teachings already exists within you; the Path is simply remembering what you already innately know.

# PART I

# *THREE MARKS OF EXISTENCE*

## — Wisdom Gained —

The Buddha realized that all the conditioned phenomena we experience in the unenlightened state have three qualities, or marks of existence: impermanence, suffering, and not-self.

You can think of conditioned phenomena as everything that is subject to and arises from cause and effect. Conditioned phenomena include everything that exists in the world and in space, all living beings including ourselves, and all mental activity. But it does not include Nirvana, the enlightened state, which transcends causes and conditions.

The Three Marks of Existence lay the groundwork for the Buddha's teachings on liberation from suffering, since those teachings describe the conditions that we experience on the path to liberation. Once we start to understand them, we can genuinely deepen our exploration and practice.

# CHAPTER I

# Anicca

## (Impermanence)

In this chapter, we will explore what impermanence really means, including the lessons we can draw from it.

## What Is Anicca?

The first mark of existence is impermanence, or *anicca* (ah-NEE-chuh). Anicca means that all conditioned phenomena, including ourselves, come into being, change continuously while existing for a period of time, and then fall away or dissolve. In essence, nothing is permanent.

We can witness the truth of anicca when we observe the leaves on the trees changing with the seasons. If you were to carefully study a single leaf from the same tree each day for a year, you would observe that as the days pass, the color, texture, and shape of the leaf alter. Each day, a somewhat new version of the leaf would appear, taking the place of the version you saw before.

We might also consider the body in this way. We know now that the majority of the cells that make up our bodies regenerate themselves over time. New cells grow to replace cells that die away. Although some of our cells will be with us for life, the majority of our cells are replaced with new ones. This means that much of the literal physical body is continually replaced with new versions of itself throughout our lifespan.

Anicca is reflected in our bodies on a larger scale as well through the processes of aging, growing sick, and dying. Even as our cells regenerate, the body accumulates wear and tear, grows frail, and eventually begins to deteriorate. Every living being will experience aging and death; there are none who will escape this.

Anicca applies to internal mental and emotional events as well. These internal phenomena can be pleasant, neutral, or unpleasant. They often appear, perhaps flutter within our awareness, and then fall away, making way for new phenomena to arise.

Everything around and within us is constantly breathing and morphing with the flow of time, always an unfolding process. Existence as we know it has never paused or remained static. We now know that even objects that appear totally solid and still are actually made up of countless rapidly moving particles. All conditioned phenomena are emerging into existence, dancing through time, and then vanishing, returning to formlessness. Like a flowing stream, everything and everyone that we will ever experience is by its very nature impermanent.

## Lessons from Anicca

What practical conclusions can we draw from anicca? We often interact with the world as if the objects and experiences we encounter will be that way forever. When we are in a bad mood or experiencing pain, the mind can convince us that this is how things will always be. When we feel euphoric, we might cling to the experience, wanting it to last as long as possible.

Anicca invites us to consider the unavoidable end of the phenomena we experience in the very moments we witness their arising. We might do so by contemplating simple questions such as, "Can I sense that this experience is changing and will eventually pass?"

Or, "This moment won't last forever; can I appreciate exactly how it feels to experience it now?"

Anicca illuminates the preciousness of life by making its transitory nature more vivid. It can serve as a catalyst for mindfulness, a teaching we will later explore as a stage on the path to liberation. When we know that no moment quite like the one happening *right here* and *right now* will *ever* occur again, we might observe a natural inclination to revel in every aspect of the moment's beauty and complexity.

The teaching of impermanence also serves as an important training in letting go. As we will learn in the chapters on the Four Noble Truths, suffering arises out of our attachment and clinging to phenomena that are impermanent, in our inability to accept anicca. By intentionally considering impermanence, we are invited to loosen our grip on things that we want to last forever. We are invited to expand our capacity for changing conditions and fleeting experiences.

Contemplating anicca can be especially challenging in relation to the people we love. Until we have lost someone close to us, we may not acknowledge their inevitable approaching death, yet it *will* happen; it is guaranteed. Every being whom we love and cherish will one day die. For most, this realization can lead to feelings of sadness, despair, fear, or even panic. We might experience similar resistance when contemplating the anicca of our own bodies. Yet all the while, our inevitable cessation is slowly approaching.

Reflecting on the truth of anicca can be a grieving process. As social and emotional creatures, it is incredibly painful for us to reflect on and accept separation from our loved ones and the fleeting home of our own bodies. It's not necessary, though, to dive into such emotionally intense contemplations headfirst.

A teaching that causes us unmanageable distress won't be particularly useful, especially for those who have experienced trauma or mental health challenges. If reading about anicca feels overwhelming, reflect on a more encouraging element of anicca's truth: the experiences that make us uncomfortable are also temporary! If we experience chronic pain, anicca invites us to observe how the pain changes in subtle ways from moment to moment and day to day. If we have ever feared an uncomfortable experience will last forever, anicca offers us the freedom of knowing that it, too, will pass.

# CHAPTER 2

# Dukkha
## (Suffering)

In this chapter, we will explore what suffering really means, including the lessons we can draw from it.

## What Is Dukkha?

The second mark of existence, dukkha (DOO-kah) in Pali, can be translated to dissatisfaction, suffering, disease, or stress. This teaching, like anicca, applies to all conditioned phenomena. It means that everything and everyone that we experience (aside from the unconditioned phenomenon of Nirvana) ultimately cannot bring us lasting contentment.

In a general sense, dukkha refers to the ongoing discomfort of being a human. Dukkha can feel like physical pain, frustration, sadness, exhaustion, annoyance, hunger, depression, and countless other distressing physical, mental, and emotional states. These experiences often come about when we are in the presence of something we dislike, hate, or have great aversion to, or when we are separated from something we like or love.

But then, we might wonder, what about the moments of great happiness in life? Can dukkha be present then? The teachings say yes, *all* conditioned phenomena are marked by dukkha.

As humans, we desire happiness and seek it in all kinds of things: friends, relationships, entertainment, pleasure, and beauty. The problem is that all of these things are conditioned phenomena, which we have now learned are subject to anicca. They do not last. Unless we are regularly contemplating and working with the truth of anicca, we go on desiring and clinging to all the conditioned phenomena that make us feel good temporarily. All the while, some part of us senses and knows from experience that the objects of our desires are always on their way out the door. So even when trying to enjoy the company of a friend, a good cup of coffee, or a relaxing day off work, dukkha slips in as resistance to the eventual end of our positive experience.

What this teaching of dukkha is getting at is that nothing will bring about liberation, or true lasting contentment, besides Nirvana. Until we awaken as the Buddha did, we will go on seeking fulfillment in impermanent, conditioned phenomena and continue the cycles of dukkha.

One such cycle specifically named by the Buddha is the cycle of birth, death, and rebirth, or *samsāra*. Upon recalling countless past lives, Buddha Gautama declared that birth itself, the process of causes and conditions luring or forcing one to be reborn into the material world as well as physical birth itself, is dukkha. After birth, as beings, we continue on toward death, all the while craving more and more life. And when death comes, whether we physically suffer or not, the forcible separation from the bodies that we so cherish is also dukkha.

Overall, identifying with bodies that are impermanent and dreading our departure from these bodies feels unstable. Existing within our conditioned human forms and being subject to constant change is unsettling and keeps us from settling into contentment. Until we reach Nirvana, dukkha will continue to inescapably pervade our experience.

# Lessons from Dukkha

Discovering the teaching of dukkha can feel discouraging or over-whelming, but there is much to be gained from reflecting on this mark of existence. Although it may seem counterintuitive, dukkha does not mean that all is hopeless, or even that we necessarily need to give up all pleasurable experiences.

Instead, try thinking of dukkha as a constant reminder to engage in dharma practice. Dukkha tells us that the only phenomenon that can actually offer us lasting contentment is Nirvana—spiritual awak-ening. As we contemplate this truth, either in meditation or daily life, we may observe a gradual loosening of how we impulsively seek happiness in impermanent, conditioned phenomena. We may also start to feel naturally motivated to meditate. This could derive from a curiosity to "try out" the teaching of dukkha and see if we can observe it ourselves, or to see if we can touch into the true, lasting contentment that Buddha said awaits in Nirvana.

Our understanding of dukkha also has practical application to navigating daily life in samsāra. One classic parable attributed to the Buddha says that an initial experience of dukkha is similar to being shot by an arrow. Quickly following the first arrow comes a second arrow: the mental and emotional reaction to the first arrow, which also consists of dukkha. By contemplating and engaging with dukkha, we can begin to work more skillfully with the layers of dukkha we add to experiences of suffering: second, third, fourth arrows, and so on. It is important to keep in mind that working on reactivity and self-regulation in this way can be aided by work-ing with a mental health professional, especially as we integrate dukkha from past experiences.

The teaching of the truth of dukkha can also help us move beyond our own individual dissatisfaction with the people around us by helping us connect to the common humanity of the experi-ence of suffering. As we reflect on the universality of dukkha, we may notice relief from the pressure to try to live the "perfect life" or be happy all the time. As we realize that every conscious being is wading through dukkha all the time, it may become clear that there is nothing wrong with you, or me, or any other living being experiencing suffering. We are *all* trapped in the cycle of samsāra, all seeking happiness in impermanent unstable phenomena, and all experiencing dukkha.

As we reflect in this way, we may notice a quivering arise in the Heartspace, a feeling of sensing into the suffering of others. In Buddhist teaching, this quivering of the heart is referred to as *karuṇā* or compassion: the heartfelt wish for others (and one-self) to be free from suffering. In the chapter about the four *brahma-viharas* (page 121), we dive deeper into this immeasurable quality of the awakened heart. For now, we can simply observe if it arises as we contemplate the teaching of dukkha. As humans in the realm of samsāra, we know what it's like to suffer and how hard it is to get free from it; we are naturally connected and feel empathy for other living beings and don't want others to suffer either. Dukkha leads us to experience the compassionate heart.

# CHAPTER 3

# Anattā
## (Not-Self)

In this chapter, we will explore the meaning of not-self, including the lessons we can draw from it.

## What Is Anattā?

The third characteristic intrinsic to all phenomena is not-self or *anattā* (AH-nuh-tuh), the lack of a solid, independently existing self. The only mark of existence that applies to both conditioned and unconditioned phenomena (Nirvana), anattā is the mark of existence that many beginners or new practitioners find to be most confusing. Anattā builds directly upon anicca (impermanence) and dukkha (suffering), so if you haven't spent time with those marks of existence, I recommend you reread and contemplate them first.

Anattā points directly to the impermanent nature of conditioned phenomena as well as the fact that we as sentient beings, unable to maintain awareness of anicca, experience constant dukkha as we try to navigate existence as though it were solid and permanent. Anattā means that because all conditioned phenomena are actually constantly unfolding processes, nothing exists as a static, complete object on its own. Even though we perceive an "I" that stays the same from moment to moment, this is an illusion of the mind. Everything, including the "self" that we experience, is actually a flowing process entirely dependent on other processes in order to exist. When referring to the "self" experienced by sentient beings, this teaching is called anattā.

Does anattā mean we don't exist? In a way, yes, and in a way, no; Buddha never answered this question outright. It means that our perception of our personality or identity is created by the mind detecting patterns in the way our processes unfold. The mind then creates the perception of an independently existing self that receives experiences, when in reality there are only countless unfolding and layered processes. This means that if we could expand our awareness of the processes that make up our perception of the self, we would eventually see that they are also intertwined with everything else: all other living beings and the world around us. In fact, nothing at all has an inherent "self" or essence. Everything that exists is a series of dependently arising processes, forever unfolding and in motion. As anattā points us to, there is no individual being within us looking out at this unfolding, because we are not separate from it.

One way we might make sense of anattā is to consider the imagery of a window. The mind constructs perception to feel like we are an individual experiencing life by peering through a window, looking on to the outside world. Anattā teaches us that actually, we *are* the window, and it is continuous with the world we are looking at. We are all windows connected to one another and the world we are navigating, not separate individuals looking out.

So, you may be wondering, why do we experience the perception of an individual identity? The Buddha described five aggregates, or *khandhas*, that make up a sentient being's sense of self. These five aggregates are material form, sensations, perceptions, mental activity, and consciousness. Material form or *rūpa* refers to the body. Sensation or *vedanā* is also sometimes translated as feeling; it refers to the sense-experience of form and its tone as either pleasant, unpleasant, or neutral. Perceptions capture the labeling aspect of the mind (for example, the color green) while mental activity refers to other mind formations like thinking and planning. Consciousness refers to our general discerning awareness.

Khandhas are also impermanent, dependently arising processes with no inherent essence and cause dukkha, but together they create the illusion of a sense of self. It is said that when Nirvana is reached, we no longer identify with these five composites; we become liberated from the sense of self, and fully realize anattā.

## Lessons from Anattā

Assuming that we are open to receiving the teaching of anattā, what do we do with such a radical notion? How do we understand and apply it in the context of daily life?

First, let's remember that anattā can be confusing and challenging to fathom. Recall Ehipassiko. come and see for yourself. We need not believe anattā on faith alone; if it does not make sense at this time, let us simply be open to seeing anattā arise in meditation or daily life, and revisit it occasionally.

Second, while we might gain secondary "lessons" from our realization of anattā, it is also sometimes considered to be one and the same as Nirvana. In other words, a full realization of anattā can be considered equivalent to awakening. So, we need not fret about anattā's various implications and can instead focus on achieving an embodied understanding of it.

We might begin to play with the notion of anattā by tuning into the fluidity of the self over time. How do you see yourself in different contexts throughout the day? How do you perceive of yourself in the workplace? With friends? At home alone? Do you have different characteristics or identity markers depending on your environment and role?

We might also practice divesting our identification with the five aggregates by observing the processes that manifest and arise in the context of anicca. For example, "I tend to experience aversion when I smell fish," rather than, "I don't like the smell of fish," or, "There is a sensation of heat," rather than, "I'm hot." As you make these minute shifts, see if any new awareness or understanding arises in turn.

As we begin to sense anattā, over time the grip loosens on our wants and desired outcomes, especially those based in entirely self-oriented motivations. One of the processes that contributes to the sense of self is the evolutionary drive for survival, the feeling that *my* continuation and well-being are the most important things, and far more important than those of any other sentient being. We can gently erode the perception of a permanent self by observing and questioning this internal drive. What makes me more important than the countless other living beings? If I were to always get what I want, what would that accomplish? We should proceed with such reflections lightly, taking care to not deny ourselves basic needs and comforts. After all, a body or nervous system that is neglected or abused is not the ideal vessel for awakening!

Finally, anattā leads us to a sense of deep interconnectedness with other living beings and the world around us. As the sense of self dissipates and we are left with interdependent processes, the boundaries separating self from other disappear. No longer are we separate, independently existing islands. If letting go of the sense of self feels overwhelming at times, let us also feel the comfort of knowing that we belong to the whole, something much greater than any single "self."

# Defending the Not-Self

Imagine for a moment that you're in a social interaction, speaking with friends or coworkers, and in the exchange, someone makes a statement that makes you feel misunderstood. Maybe someone responds to you in a way that demonstrates they misinterpreted something you shared. Maybe someone makes a generalization about you that does not feel true to who you are. Or perhaps someone shares something about you that is simply not true. How do you react?

In such situations, it is expected that you might feel offended, angry, hurt, or defensive. You might defend yourself or make an argument about why the statement is not true. You might even raise your voice or crinkle your eyebrows in disgust. Alternatively, you might feel inclined to leave the situation altogether.

While it is important for us to take care of ourselves and set appropriate boundaries with others, a situation such as this is also an ideal practice space for working with the Three Marks of Existence.

We might most obviously observe dukkha in this situation. It usually does not feel good to be misunderstood, and the second arrows of reactive emotions that follow also feel uncomfortable. As we observe the unfolding of dukkha in such situations, we simply label it: "There's dukkha . . . there's dukkha . . . oh, there's more dukkha." By seeing and naming suffering for what it is—a universally experienced mark of existence—our resistance to it may lessen.

By observing dukkha, we might find comfort in recalling anicca: although uncomfortable experiences are arising now, they are temporary. They will soon fade away and make way for a different experience. I will not feel this way forever. The Sufi phrase "this too shall pass" is sometimes helpful for recalling anicca in difficult moments.

And finally, such a situation is perfect for contemplating anattā. Who is it that feels misunderstood? What is the nature of this supposedly true-self that has not been properly seen? Why does it feel so offended by the misperception? What would it mean if the perception was actually true? Anattā invites us to gently probe the assumptions that we make every day, especially in situations such as this, about who we are.

By bringing the Three Marks of Existence into such common social situations, we may begin to feel a lessening of our reactivity and concern about being perceived a certain way. When we realize that the self is actually a flexible, impermanent collection of processes, and that our feelings are normal, universal, and don't last forever, the intensity of such difficult moments lessens and makes way for more ease.

## LABELING THE AGGREGATES

Labeling is a useful tool for giving names to the components that make up experience. By labeling some observed aspects of the five aggregates, as in this body and sensation scan exercise, we can begin to let go of the idea of a permanent self.

Sit comfortably on a cushion or chair. Close your eyes or cast the eyes downward. Take a few breaths to come into the body and sink into your seat.

Begin by observing the *body*. You might slowly scan your awareness from your toes up to the top of the head. You might especially notice the movement of breathing or the heartbeat. Label or note each experience you observe as "form," "body," or "matter."

Scan the body again, this time observing any *sensations* you observe as the body interacts with the environment. Pause to note any sensations that catch your attention along the way: pain, warmth, coolness, itchiness, or contact with the seat. Label all your observations as "sensation" or "feeling." You might also label them as "pleasant," "neutral," or "unpleasant."

Finally, turn your attention inward to the mind. What do you observe arising? Note any thoughts, planning, memories, or daydreaming, and label them "mental formations."

Repeat this labeling until the mind settles and begins to let go of its observed experience.

# PART II

# *THE FOUR NOBLE TRUTHS*

## — Wisdom Gained —

It is thought that the Four Noble Truths were the first teachings given by the Buddha, the great healer of the world, after he achieved enlightenment. The idea of Buddha as physician or healer comes from the medicinal approach of the Four Noble Truths. The first truth, dukkha or suffering, is the clinical observation of the human condition. The second truth, the cause of dukkha, is the diagnosis. The third truth, the cessation of dukkha, is the prognosis. The fourth truth, the path to freedom from dukkha, is the treatment or cure. These truths build directly upon the Three Marks of Existence, and give way to the Noble Eightfold Path to liberation.

# CHAPTER 4

# The Truth of Suffering

In this chapter, we will explore the meaning of the truth of suffering, including the lessons we can draw from it.

## What Is the Truth of Suffering?

Like the second mark of existence, the first noble truth is dukkha. Dukkha can be translated as suffering, dissatisfaction, pain, or distress. Recall that dukkha points directly at anicca, or the impermanent nature of conditioned phenomena. The truth of suffering is that sentient existence is marked by the inability to feel satisfied or content by the ever-changing everyday phenomena we navigate.

In his discourse on the Four Noble Truths, Buddha explains that dukkha manifests as the physical experiences of birth, aging, illness, death, and rebirth. Recall that together these form the cycle or realm of samsāra.

Buddha said that birth is both physically and spiritually painful for a new being entering this world. It also gives way to inevitable aging, sickness, and death and therefore, as a cause of suffering, cannot be separated from suffering itself. Aging and illness as dukkha refer to both the physical pain of existing in a deteriorating body and the existential helplessness of being continuously subject to progressive aging and disease. Similarly, death as dukkha refers to both the experience of dying often as overtly painful along with the anticipation of parting with the beloved body and all the accompanying unknowns associated with such a transition.

Buddha explains that dukkha also manifests as mental and emotional states, specifically naming sorrow, lamentation, grief, and despair as dukkha. We might also consider experiences like anger, frustration, irritation, restlessness, exhaustion, self-consciousness, and anxiety. Whether getting upset about spilling coffee on our way to work or grieving the loss of a loved one, all these kinds of unpleasant internal experiences are considered dukkha.

Buddha also explained that, more generally, whenever we interact with something we hate or dislike, like spending time with someone we don't get along with, going to the dentist, or eating a food we don't enjoy, that is also dukkha. Similarly, whenever we are separated from something we like or love or simply do not get what we want, that, too, is dukkha. This could be missing family who live far away, misplacing our keys or cell phone, or not getting the promotion we expected. We are beings seeking permanent happiness trapped in a realm marked by anicca, and therefore also dukkha.

Buddha concludes the teachings on the first noble truth by explaining that the five aggregates, or khandhas, are themselves also dukkha. Recall that the khandhas (material form, sensations, perceptions, mental activity, and consciousness) are the five material and mental components that contribute to the sense of self. We tend to identify with and cling to these khandhas. We think of the body as "my body" and the patterns in the way we think, speak, and behave as "my personality." And yet, the khandhas are also marked by anicca, so they, too, constitute dukkha.

We should also remember that even moments of pleasure and joy in life are not separate from dukkha. These experiences, like all else, are transient and changing, and so they are incapable of providing lasting satisfaction. We might enjoy riding a roller coaster while the ride is in motion, but the mind interacts with the experience as if it can bring us lasting contentment, and soon enough the ride is over, leaving us wanting more.

The discourse that explains these different aspects of dukkha, called the *Dhammacakkappavattana Sutta*, is sometimes translated as "the setting in motion of the wheel of dharma" sutta, or alternatively "the establishment of the wheel of truth" sutta. By offering this sermon that begins with the nature of suffering inherent in the human condition, Buddha establishes the foundation for offering the spiritual cure to our distress.

## Lessons from the Truth of Suffering

Reflecting on the first noble truth can feel upsetting or difficult to process, but it does not mean we should give up hope for joy in this life. Let us recall that teachings are only useful to us to the extent that we can interact with them effectively. Buddha taught differently depending on whom he was teaching. The teachings offered might be more or less intellectually complex, or have different focuses depending on a student's needs. So, as we interact with intense teachings such as the noble truth of suffering, let us be skillful in assessing whether or not it is serving us. If we notice that we become overwhelmingly anxious, depressed, or hopeless upon contemplating dukkha, we should set it aside for a while and direct attention to a teaching that feels more easeful to reflect on.

That said, if we can hold the truth of dukkha lightly, approaching it with a sense of curiosity and embodied, nonjudgmental awareness, we might gain some clarity about how dukkha manifests in our lives and experiences. We might, for example, observe what it feels like to see gray hairs in the mirror, to witness our own aging. What arises in the body and mind? We might also immerse in the experience of discomfort when we take a bite of a food with a flavor we don't enjoy. Can we pinpoint feelings of aversion or disgust?

When we engage in such contemplations, we can begin to work with the cycles that potentiate dukkha in our everyday lives. We can use the noble truth of suffering to practice seeing things as they really are, recognizing in any given experience how dukkha is manifesting, and beginning to know this noble truth for ourselves.

We might then also reflect on any second or third arrows (page 11) that arise when we observe dukkha (things like shame, fear, anxiety, or discomfort) and see those experiences as they are as well. After taking that bite of the food we don't enjoy, do we observe shame about being a picky eater? Do we observe annoyance with whoever made the food? Frustration with the fact that healthy foods don't taste as delicious as unhealthy foods do?

We don't need to judge ourselves in our experiences of and reactions to dukkha. With awareness, we gain clarity about the true nature of things and we slowly begin to see the cycles of suffering in everyday life diminish. This is covered in more detail in part 3 of the book (page 53).

While some practitioners believe we should divest from all pleasant experiences because of dukkha, it isn't necessary to do so. Sensory experiences (*vedanā-khandha*) are felt as pleasant, unpleasant, or neutral, so even intentionally avoiding pleasant experiences does not free us from the need to learn to skillfully interact with different kinds of experiences, all of which are dukkha.

CHAPTER 5

# The Truth of the
# Cause of Suffering

In this chapter, we will explore the meaning of the cause of
suffering, including the lessons we can draw from it.

## What Is the Truth of the Cause of Suffering?

You may well be asking yourself: Why so much dukkha? What is
it about the way we interact with our impermanent realities that
creates dukkha? The second noble truth is the truth of the cause
of dukkha: craving or *tanhā*, which can also be translated to thirst,
longing, or desire.

Taṇhā can be broken down into three major types of craving
that bind us to dukkha and samsāra. *Kāma-taṇhā* refers to craving for sensual pleasures. It includes the longing and attachment
we experience for pleasant feelings that arise from food, wealth,
drugs, and relationships, as well as more abstract things like power,
ideals, and views. Perhaps it is clear how craving for such imperma
nent objects of desire leads us to dukkha; although we have brief
experiences of pleasure or even fulfillment upon attaining these
objects, this enjoyment never lasts and we are left with the same
longing, and the same dukkha.

*Bhava-taṇhā* means craving to be. This type of craving can refer to the desire for life, the attachment to our identities, and the ego's ongoing striving to establish and maintain itself. It can also refer to our longing for eternal life after death, the desire to carry on being in our current form. We have already explored how we, as sentient beings, are not separate from conditioned phenomena, and therefore are subject to anicca. Our bodies, minds, and identities are impermanent, but our craving for being is bound to create dukkha.

The third type of craving is *vibhava-taṇhā*, or craving for nonexistence. This refers to a desire for any experience to go away or end. It could be as simple as wishing your annoying neighbor would stop talking to you, or as dark and complex as wanting to end your life. Vibhava-taṇhā is the rejection of something that is arising and craving its absence instead.

Together, these three types of taṇhā make up the origin of dukkha. Buddha taught that in addition to creating the basis for all immediate experiences of dukkha, taṇhā is also the primary cause of samsāra itself. Our entire world and all the sentient beings that inhabit it exist because of the longing for manifestation. And so, the cycles of rebirth and dukkha will continue as long as taṇhā reigns.

## Lessons from the Truth of the Cause of Suffering

How might we incorporate an understanding of taṇhā as the origin of dukkha? We cannot simply turn off our desires, nor should we attempt such an absolute approach. Instead, we might receive the second noble truth as an invitation to observe the connection between craving and dissatisfaction.

When we experience frustration, it's worth asking ourselves what we wish was different. When we feel annoyed with a person or situation, what would we prefer? In a happy or exciting moment, can we detect a longing for the experience to last indefinitely? The second noble truth invites us to examine the link between that which we crave and the dukkha that follows our cravings.

The truth of the cause of suffering also offers a unique insight into how we fail to grasp anattā, not-self. This truth tells us that one of the three types of craving is craving for being. We cling to our five aggregates, identities, personalities, individuality, and sense of self, although we now know that the true nature of all phenomena is anattā. As we have explored, everything, including ourselves, is a series of interdependent processes in motion, and yet bhava-taṇhā keeps us thoroughly committed to our individual identities. The second noble truth reveals the force that keeps us from realizing anattā.

Reflection upon the second noble truth can also lead to a more practical reminder. Desire often implies a wish for attainment or possession of something. Attainment and possession not only further solidify a sense of self but also indicate a degree of selfishness. Our wishes for attainment (for example, possessing certain objects or people, to go on living indefinitely, or to avoid anything we do not like) reveal an aspect of our self-construction that places the self in the center of the universe. When we are driven by desire, no one else's wishes compare in terms of magnitude of importance. Even when we have benevolent wishes for the benefit of others, our attachment to that view as the *right one* reveals a self-centered framework.

Such an ego-centered orientation only leads to more dukkha; this self and all its desires are only impermanent aspects of conditioned phenomena. The importance and relevance of the self and its wishes will never be realized because their true nature is anattā. So, how do we handle realization of the selfishness of our constant taṇhā?

As individuals conditioned in our competitive and individualistic broader society, our first reaction may be one of shame or self-judgment. This, too, is just another sneaky manifestation of the craving self, seeking comfort in its own being. As we contemplate the second noble truth and all that it implies about the nature of the self and its desires, let us simply bring kind, nonjudgmental awareness. Let us observe how the self creates layers and layers of wanting and reactivity without judging it. In contemplating the noble truths, the intention is merely to practice seeing their truth in our own experience. Ehipassiko, come and see for yourself.

# CHAPTER 6

# The Truth of the Freedom from Suffering

In this chapter, we will explore the meaning of freedom from suffering, including the lessons we can draw from it.

## What Is the Truth of the Freedom from Suffering?

The third noble truth offers a great dose of encouragement after the seemingly bleak first and second truths: it is the truth of the freedom from suffering, the end of dukkha.

But how could it be that one of the marks of all conditioned phenomena has an end? Does dukkha not manifest in every human experience we have? In this truth, Buddha reveals that if we can understand a phenomenon's causes, that phenomenon also has an end. The second noble truth taught us that dukkha's cause is craving, and thus dukkha has an end. That end arises when we let go of desire, and is called Nirvana.

Nirvana is said to be the only unconditioned phenomenon in existence. It is a state of awakening, understanding, and liberation. It is also said that Nirvana is comprised of total peace and perfect lasting joy. In other words, it is what we all *ultimately* long for, and mistakenly look for in our impermanent world.

Nirvana is also described as the end of samsāra. Those who reach the far shores of Nirvana are liberated from the cycle of rebirth. They may choose to be born again to stay on Earth and assist other living beings on their journeys to liberation, but they are not drawn back to rebirth by compulsion.

Nirvana can be translated from Pali as "to blow out," and this translation refers to the extinguishing of the fires of taṇhā or craving. When our craving and clinging fade away once and for all, what remains is Nirvana: our true nature. In this truth, Buddha revealed that at the deepest level, despite our faults, cravings, and delusions of self, our true nature is the undefiled perfection of Nirvana. This is sometimes called Buddha-nature.

This is a vital concept to sit with. *Our true nature is Nirvana.* Buddha-nature is not something that we must build or manifest. It is there all the time beneath the craving and suffering. Even though dukkha is one of the marks of existence, it is not the ultimate nature of existence. It is like a cloud obscuring our view of the vast blue sky. When we are able to work skillfully with the causes of the dukkha clouds, the Nirvana sky will still be there and is indeed always there, peering out from behind the clouds and waiting to be revealed.

The third noble truth gifts us the profound realization that when craving ends, suffering will end; both are impermanent and when they pass, the true nature of Nirvana will be revealed. Upon reaching this state, one is fully liberated from all dukkha: uncomfortable emotional states, aging, sickness, and even death and rebirth; one is set free from the realm of samsāra and rests in perfect knowing and awareness.

# Lessons from the Truth of the Freedom from Suffering

What would it look like to realize the third noble truth in our modern world? How can we imagine letting go of our desires for pleasure, friends, family, good health, wealth, and even our own lives? How could that possibly lead to freedom? The steps that Buddha outlines as the path to liberation are explored in more detail in the chapters on the Noble Eightfold Path. For now, let us simply reflect on the knowing of this truth.

The second noble truth taught us to begin observing the connection between desires and suffering. This third noble truth offers us an invitation to begin to consider what freedom might look like. Perhaps we have been working on watching dukkha arise when we are in craving, or started tracing dukkha back to desires we were holding. Let us now begin playing with the possibility of ending this cycle of craving and suffering.

Imagination is a useful tool in Buddhist practice. When we are so embedded in the samsaric cycles of suffering, it can be hard to conceive of a reality that is different. How can we make sense of a state of being that is so vastly different from the day-to-day we are used to? This third noble truth offers us the opportunity to start with our observations here and now: to observe how our clinging is leading to suffering, and to *imagine* what it would be like to no longer cling.

So, as we contemplate this noble truth and the end of suffering, let us begin to imagine in our daily lives what would happen if our desires lessened. We need not even begin with imagining letting a desire go entirely; we can simply imagine it lessening in intensity. For example, the next time we feel an intense desire to watch our favorite TV show and perhaps experience dukkha if we cannot watch it immediately, let us explore the third noble truth by imagining what it would be like if that craving were not so intense.

This is not an intellectual game of figuring out how to talk ourselves out of the desire, or wondering why we have the desire, or shaming ourselves for having the desire. We are simply imagining a world in which the desire is less persistent. What would that feel like? How would our experience of dukkha be affected? By allowing ourselves to play make-believe in this way, we are actually opening the mind to help it better perceive the third noble truth. We are bridging the gap between samsāra and Nirvana.

If this approach does not feel accessible, we might also simply contemplate the lovely encouragement that this truth offers us. *The cessation of our suffering is possible*. Dukkha is not forever. We might simply sit with this idea and allow ourselves to feel the hope and joy of the possibility of liberation. Such positive emotions will help fuel us as we embark on the Noble Eightfold Path to freedom.

# CHAPTER 7

# The Truth of the Path of Liberation from Suffering

In this chapter, we will explore the meaning of liberation from suffering, including the lessons we can draw from it and a useful anecdote to ground these concepts. We'll finish with a meditation practice to bring us closer to the path of liberation from suffering.

## What Is the Truth of the Path of Liberation from Suffering?

The fourth noble truth presents the cure to the ailment of dukkha: the path of liberation from suffering. This teaching is sometimes also translated as *the noble truth of the way of practice leading to the cessation of suffering*. It describes what the Buddha called the Noble Eightfold Path.

This path to liberation is made up of eight components of practice that together free us from the causes of dukkha: taṇhā. By following this path, our self-oriented desires and cravings are extinguished, making way to awaken our true Buddha-nature.

The stages of the Noble Eightfold Path are:

- Right view
  (or right understanding)
- Right intention
- Right speech
- Right action
- Right livelihood
- Right effort
- Right mindfulness
- Right concentration

Each of these stages is explored in greater detail in part 3 of the book (page 53); here we touch on each of them briefly so that we may contemplate the fourth noble truth.

**Right view**, sometimes also called **right understanding**, refers to a grounding in the realization of both the Three Marks of Existence and the Four Noble Truths. Although generally the components of the Path do not need to be followed in order, right view is often considered the foundation for all other aspects of the Path. It gives us a sense of where we are starting (samsāra marked by dukkha caused by taṇhā) and where we are going (liberation in Nirvana, reached via the Noble Eightfold Path). We cultivate right view by contemplating and meditating on the Three Marks of Existence and Four Noble Truths such that we have a clear perspective for practice.

**Right intention** is also sometimes referred to as right resolve, purpose, or thought. Buddha specifically names intentions of renunciation (letting go of worldly things), freedom from ill will, and harmlessness. Right intention brings clarity to the mind about the direction of spiritual practice.

**Right speech** is the ethical training of divesting from lying, rudeness, deception, and gossip.

**Right action or conduct** is the ethical training of divesting from killing or injuring other living beings, stealing, sexual misconduct, and unwise use of intoxicants.

**Right livelihood or occupation** is the ethical training of engaging in ethical, honest work to support oneself.

**Right effort** is the mental training of the cultivation of wholesome energy and states of mind and the guarding against unwholesome states of mind. Right effort is guided by right view and right intention. It includes exertion, diligence, and perseverance.

**Right mindfulness** (*sati*) or attention is the mental training in the cultivation of calm, curious, nonjudgmental awareness of the present moment.

**Right concentration** (*samādhi* or *jhāna*) is mental training in the cultivation of composed, one-pointed concentration.

It is important to note that these factors do not have to be realized in sequence; they do not follow a linear progression of practice. However, they do build upon one another, and at times aspects of one factor are supportive to another factor. Altogether, these eight factors mutually support one another to form the whole path of practice that leads to liberation.

## Lessons from the Truth of the Path of Liberation from Suffering

What should we take with us from the fourth noble truth? This teaching is a profound gift from the Buddha that outlines precisely how he journeyed from samsāra to Nirvana. By offering us the truth of the path of practice, Buddha gives us the power to awaken as well.

In the next several chapters, we will explore each stage of the Noble Eightfold Path in depth. For now, we can begin to contemplate the Path as a whole.

The Noble Eightfold Path can be broken down into three major sections: ethics (*sīla*), concentration (samādhi), and wisdom (*paññā*) trainings.

The section of the Path pertaining to ethics is sometimes called the moral discipline group; this group is made up of right speech, right action, and right livelihood. These are often considered the first division of the Path, and the basis for the concentration aspects. Why might this be the case?

The trainings in ethics are based on the concept of *kamma*, often referred to as karma: that all intentions and actions become causes for future effects, both for ourselves and for others. This applies to both the conditions we experience in this life (for example, the more we indulge in sugar, the more likely we are to continue indulging in sugar in the future), and across lives (for example, if we cultivate good karma in this life, then we are more likely to experience a favorable rebirth in the next life).

We train in moral discipline to cultivate the conditions that will be most encouraging to further awakening, for ourselves and for all other living beings. We therefore practice speaking only what is true, kind, and necessary; engaging in wholesome actions; and earning a living in an ethical manner.

The second group within the Path is the concentration group consisting of right effort, right mindfulness, and right concentration. These are built upon moral discipline and form the foundation for wisdom training.

With these three components, we progress from ethical training in the outer world to training the mind in the inner world. The goal of these three aspects is a still, focused mind that can rest completely in awareness. Right effort brings energy to this goal, right mindfulness offers awareness, and right concentration brings equanimity and one-pointed focus. These components are sometimes said to focus on training a higher consciousness that can hold the truths realized in the wisdom trainings.

The third division of the Path is the wisdom or insight group, made up of right view and right intention. This group is both the starting place and culmination of the Path. We begin with these trainings by understanding why the Path should be followed and complete the Path with total insight into the nature of things.

How is wisdom cultivated? Wisdom here does not refer to knowledge gained from studying but to insight that spontaneously arises when the causes and conditions are right. This is why moral discipline and concentration trainings are necessary foundations to the wisdom trainings.

So, once again, we can sense the encouragement and empowerment of knowing that our choices and engagement with practice are leading us to liberation.

# The Noble Truths of Traffic

Imagine that you are sitting in traffic. It's been bumper-to-bumper for miles and there is no end in sight. Maybe there's an accident or major construction, or maybe it's just rush hour. The next exit is several miles ahead, and you are late to your destination.

To top it all off, two lanes are merging into one and a couple of vehicles surge past you on the shoulder, forcing their way into your lane and cutting you off.

This is likely an experience that many of us have struggled with, and such a situation is wonderfully fertile ground for working with the Four Noble Truths.

We can begin by reflecting on the first noble truth by observing the dukkha arising. We might bring our awareness to our experience of frustration, stress, impatience, boredom, or maybe even anger or hatred. There might also be hunger or soreness in the body. Without judgment, we can simply note each of these facets of experience, labeling them as "dukkha."

We can then progress to examining the second noble truth. What are we clinging to or wanting that is creating this dukkha? Perhaps there is a desire to get to our destination within a certain time frame. Perhaps there is a desire to *not* encounter the consequences of being late to our destination, such as missing an appointment, getting in trouble or fired from a job, or not having time to relax. Or perhaps the desire is simply to *not* be stuck in a vehicle! There may be a desire to move the body, or to not have to focus on the road.

From there we can recall the third noble truth: if we can let go of our need for things to be different than how they are, the dukkha will begin to fade.

How might we do that? The fourth noble truth tells us that the answer is the Noble Eightfold Path, which we can actually practice right there in the car in the middle of the traffic jam.

Reflecting on right view, we may take steps toward realizing anattā by feeling into the importance of *others'* experiences: others in the cars around us experiencing dukkha or, if there was an accident, the suffering of those involved and their loved ones.

Cultivating right intention, we may think to ourselves, "May I work with this situation skillfully for the sake of enlightenment for all beings."

Training in right speech, we refrain from yelling or honking at other drivers. Training in right action, we allow the people who are trying to merge to enter in front of us, even if *they* do not appear to be training in moral discipline! Right action might also include taking steps to care for ourselves and our own nervous systems: taking some deep breaths, staying hydrated, or even pulling over and taking a break if we need to.

Focusing on the concentration group of the Path, we might choose to listen to a guided meditation or practice concentrating on the breath or heartbeat. As we meditate, we might open ourselves up to the wisdom factors again by simply observing if any spontaneous insights arise.

In this way, an ordinary, frustrating traffic jam becomes a training moment in the Four Noble Truths.

## SATI & THE CESSATION
## OF SUFFERING

This practice makes use of the power of imagination to open the mind to the third noble truth: the truth of the end of suffering. It can be practiced in formal seated meditation or in any given moment of daily life.

Pausing where you are, turn the awareness to the body and allow it to settle. Take a moment to notice your breathing or heartbeat with gentle, mindful awareness.

Then ask yourself, "What would it be like to experience and accept this moment exactly as it is? What would it be like to not want anything about this moment to be different?"

Sink into awareness of the present moment fully, exploring the richness of its details: sensations, thoughts, feelings. You might also greet each observation you make, especially those that are difficult. For example, "Hello, resistance," or "Welcome, distraction."

Carry on in this way for several minutes, continuously coming back to the question, "What would it be like to accept this moment exactly as it is?" Watch the craving and dukkha fall away as you allow them to be there.

# PART III

# THE NOBLE EIGHTFOLD PATH

## — Wisdom Gained —

The Noble Eightfold Path is built directly upon the Four Noble Truths and offers instructions for how to proceed given the nature of the reality we find ourselves in. The Path is made up of eight components that form the backbone of spiritual practice in the Buddhist tradition. We will investigate each in detail in the following chapters, exploring how Buddha teaches that these eight aspects of practice together lead us to awakening.

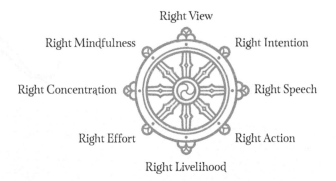

# CHAPTER 8

# Sammā-diṭṭhi
## (Right View)

In this chapter, we will explore the meaning of right view, including the lessons we can draw from it.

## What Is Right View?

The first component described on the Noble Eightfold Path is *sammā-diṭṭhi* or right view. We can also think of right view as right understanding or perspective.

*Diṭṭhi*, or view, comprises both our clearly formulated beliefs and our unconscious assumptions and ways of perceiving the world. Diṭṭhi can include culturally conditioned biases, internalized gender roles, beliefs we hold about what is right and wrong, and how we ultimately view and interpret the nature of reality. At its core, diṭṭhi refers to everything that the mind, both consciously and unconsciously, holds to be true.

And what makes a view "right"? *Sammā*, or "right," refers to a complete or correct understanding of the Buddha's teachings, principally the Four Noble Truths and the Three Marks of Existence. This means that we approach the Noble Eightfold Path with an embodied understanding of anicca, dukkha, and anattā, as well as the truths of suffering, its causes, its cessation, and the path to liberation. Therefore, studying, contemplating, and meditating upon these teachings can be practice in sammā-diṭṭhi.

Buddha also teaches that when we come to deeply know the Four Noble Truths and the Three Marks of Existence, an understanding of kamma follows. Kamma means action, specifically freely chosen and intentional action. The principle of kamma is that purposeful actions produce results that correspond and align with the actions' level of wholesomeness. Wholesome kamma are ethical and lead to freedom from suffering for oneself and others, while unwholesome kamma are unethical and lead to further suffering for oneself and others.

Kamma can be bodily actions, speech, and mental activity. All of the intentional actions taken in these three areas will lead to some corresponding results. Sammā-diṭṭhi means that we cultivate a clear and embodied understanding of the kamma that are wholesome and the kamma that are unwholesome.

Sammā-diṭṭhi does *not* mean we need to have a perfect understanding of ethics or the mechanics of the *kammic* system. It simply means we understand that when we engage in harmful actions, speech, and thoughts, they lead to further suffering for ourselves and others. Similarly, when we engage in kind actions, speech, and thoughts, they help lead ourselves and others toward liberation from suffering.

Although all eight components of the Path work together, sammā-diṭṭhi is considered a necessary starting point and guide for the other stages because a grounded understanding of the core teachings is what propels us forth on the Path and enables us to make skillful choices along the way. However, sammā-diṭṭhi is part of the wisdom or paññā group, and wisdom unfolds in stages over time. Indeed, right view also serves as the final stage for liberation from suffering: awakening.

And so, from our embodied understanding of the Three Marks of Existence, the Four Noble Truths, and the principle of kamma, we embark on the remainder of the Noble Eightfold Path.

## Lessons from Right View

Why is right view essential as both an aspect on the Eightfold Path and something to bring into our daily lives? On its own, diṭṭhi determines our attitudes, choices, and ways of being and relating to the world around us. Diṭṭhi is the mental framework that helps us make sense of our existence and decide what to do with it. Sammā-diṭṭhi is therefore the means of cultivating that mental framework that ultimately leads to liberation from suffering.

Grounded in a knowing of anicca, we begin to understand that craving is the cause of suffering. Once we see clearly that unwholesome actions lead to greater suffering, the groundwork is laid for us to divest from cycles of harmful actions. But what determines whether an action is wholesome or unwholesome? How can we discern in day-to-day life whether the choices we are making will lead to suffering or not?

In the teachings on kamma, Buddha explains that the roots of unwholesome kamma are the three poisons: greed, aversion, and delusion, also called *kleshas*, that are three aspects of taṇhā, all resulting in dukkha. Greed equates to kāma-taṇhā or craving for sense pleasure and bhava-taṇhā or craving for being, aversion equates to vibhava-taṇhā or craving for nonexistence, and delusion is the basis of all taṇhā. When we see these three poisons arising and likely affecting our actions, it is an indicator of unwholesome actions.

Imagine you are at a holiday party for work and go to get a delicious treat from the snack table. When you get to the table, you see that there is just one left, and your colleague is walking toward it. In that moment, you may see greed arise as you desire to enjoy the sensual pleasure of the treat all for yourself. But we know that greed is one of the three poisons and therefore the root of unwholesome action, so perhaps taking the treat for yourself is an unwholesome action that will only lead to further suffering for yourself and your colleague.

Similarly, you might see the poison of aversion arise when you find yourself trying to avoid an uncomfortable but much-needed confrontation with a housemate. The arising of this klesha can indicate that the action of avoiding the confrontation may be an unwholesome action that will lead to further suffering.

Taking all of this into consideration, practicing sammā-diṭṭhi by seeing our actions and their roots as wholesome or unwholesome does *not* mean we should intentionally avoid everything that is appealing to us and forcibly expose ourselves to that which is harmful. It simply means we practice seeing clearly the roots of our actions and see if we can bring awareness and right view to what is arising in each moment. By clearly seeing those unwholesome roots arising, we engage with sammā-diṭṭhi and practice the Path.

It may also be encouraging to learn that the three poisons each have opposite wholesome qualities that we can also see clearly as part of our engagement with sammā-diṭṭhi. Opposite to greed is generosity, opposite to aversion is *mettā* or loving-kindness, and opposite to delusion is wisdom. So, we can consider these three mental factors as the roots of wholesome kamma that will lead to the liberation from suffering.

In this way, sammā-diṭṭhi serves as an invitation to regularly come back to an awareness of our underlying beliefs and perceptions, whether they be wholesome or unwholesome, and what their effects might be in the realm of samsāra.

# CHAPTER 9

# Sammā-sankappa
## (Right Intention)

In this chapter, we will explore the meaning of right intention, including the lessons we can draw from it.

## What Is Right Intention?

The second factor on the Eightfold Path is *sammā-sankappa* or right intention. It can also be translated as right resolve, purpose, or thought. It refers to the aims and ideals that the mind is set upon. Situated between right view and the moral discipline group, sammā-sankappa bridges the gap between our perspective on the world and how we engage with it.

It can be helpful to think of intentions as the states or ways of being that we willingly incline our minds toward. Intentions are not goals in themselves, but they can be the manner by which we accomplish a goal. For example, we can intend to approach our tasks for the day mindfully. The intention is the mindful way of being that we aspire to point ourselves toward as we approach our everyday errands, chores, and tasks.

Buddha names three specific intentions that make up sammā-sankappa: the intention for renunciation, the intention for goodwill, and the intention for harmlessness.

Renunciation is the turning away from our worldly desires and constant seeking for satisfaction. The act of renouncing in daily life can refer to forsaking almost any earthly thing, including items and actions like drinking alcohol, eating meat, engaging in gambling, or consuming sugary foods. The intention of renunciation is about inclining the mind toward letting go.

Ending dukkha requires the elimination of craving, and we eliminate craving by directing the mind toward renunciation. We can cultivate this right intention by examining how our desires for worldly things are actually contributing to dukkha, by returning to right view. We can do so by seeing how it feels in the body to crave the things we want most—desserts, sex, money, alcohol, or another type of high. Ground in the body and observe how the longing feels. We often see quickly that we are suffering. From there we can focus on the knowing that relieving that craving with a "hit" of what we desire is inherently temporary and unwholesome, and will naturally lead to further suffering. From that place of knowing, see if an inclination toward the freedom of renunciation arises.

The intention of goodwill is a commitment to incline the mind and heart toward loving-kindness or mettā for all living beings. Mettā is the genuine selfless wish for others' well-being. It is distinguishable from romantic love and friendship love, but it can also be present in those relationships. The key aspect of mettā is selflessness. This does not mean abandoning one's own needs, but that the feeling of love is not based in a self at all, just a genuine spontaneous wish for another's welfare.

Mettā can't be forced, but it can be cultivated from the seeds of spontaneous loving-kindness that already live within each of us. Commitment to this cultivation is the right intention of goodwill. Mettā is explored further in the chapter on the brahma-viharas (page 121).

The intention of harmlessness is also a commitment to incline the mind and heart toward compassion, or karuṇā, for all living beings. Karunā is often described as mettā in the presence of suffering. It is the genuine wish for others to be free from suffering. It is important, however, that we maintain healthy boundaries around empathy. We explore those boundaries further in a later chapter (page 123). For now, we can know that our intention of harmlessness is based in the genuine wish for all beings to be free from suffering.

## Lessons from Right Intention

We can bring the three right intentions of renunciation, goodwill, and harmlessness into daily life with certain realistic everyday practices. However, we do not need to jump right to action. Recall that intentions are not goals, but instead they're ways of being that we aspire to and incline the mind toward. We might begin by simply writing down the intention to engage in one or more of these practices. In this way, we can start to spend time with these ways of being and see if the inclination begins to arise spontaneously within ourselves. If it doesn't, we shouldn't force engagement with these intentions, but merely stay open and continue to contemplate them regularly.

Some practices for cultivating the intention of renunciation are giving up meat, letting go of sugar or alcohol for periods of time, taking a break from social media or television, practicing celibacy for a period of time, or cutting or shaving one's hair. As we consider these practice ideas, remember that they do not need to be forever. We might choose a renunciation practice to engage with one day per week.

The simplest way to engage with the intention of goodwill is to bring mindfulness when mettā spontaneously arises. We might see a cute dog in our neighborhood and suddenly wish that good pup as much happiness as possible. Or perhaps we see a precious baby pass by in a stroller and hope they have a wonderful life.

When we observe such a feeling emerge, we should spend time with it. What does it feel like in the body? Can we focus on it and absorb into the experience of loving-kindness? In this way, we can realistically incline the mind toward the intention of goodwill.

Similar to mettā practice, we can bring mindfulness to spontaneous compassion that arises throughout the day to cultivate the intention of harmlessness. Perhaps we encounter an individual experiencing homelessness on our commute and find ourselves hoping they have a warm place to sleep tonight and desiring to work to end homelessness. Or maybe we see the body of a raccoon or squirrel that has been run over by a car and pray that their death was not painful. In such moments, we can draw our attention to the Heartspace and focus on the experience.

As we begin to play with right intentions in our daily lives, we may observe that the mind has a backfire effect: it does not always want to let go of that which it desires! It does not want to cultivate goodwill and harmlessness toward enemies! It is important in these moments that we do not fight with the mind or shame ourselves into right intentions. Such approaches are usually secretly based in ill will. When we encounter such internal resistance, we should return back to right view and focus on building our sense of understanding. From a place of seeing clearly, an authentic movement toward right intention arises. As our perspective on the objects of our desires change, they gradually become less attractive to us. As our perspective on the objects of our aversion change, they gradually become less offensive to us. From the seeds of right view grow the blossoms of right intentions.

# CHAPTER 10

# Sammā-vaca
## (Right Speech)

In this chapter, we will explore the meaning of right speech, including the lessons we can draw from it.

## What Is Right Speech?

The next three components of the Path, right speech, right action, and right livelihood, make up the moral discipline or sīla group. While this group of teachings is concerned with not causing harm to others, it is also about training and purifying our own minds through our behavioral choices. Unwholesome speech, actions, and livelihood do not just hurt others; they hurt us, too!

Our ethical choices must be based in right view and right intentions. They should not be interpreted as harsh command-ments to be blindly obeyed, but treated as an extension of our understanding of and commitment to spiritual practice. In fact, Buddha instructs that the moral disciplines should be practiced *before* the aspects of the Path concerning meditation (right effort, right mindfulness, and right concentration). In other words, if we have to choose between focusing on ethical conduct and sitting in meditation, we should choose ethical conduct.

The main aspects of the sīla group can be framed as abstentions ("do not lie") and as encouragements ("speak the truth"), and both are actually necessary. We must both refrain from unwholesome speech and actions as well as commit to wholesome ones. These abstentions and encouragements are often explained through the teaching of the five precepts. We explore the precepts more in the chapter on right action (page 73). For now, we will consider abstentions and their corresponding encouragements for right speech.

First, what does speech refer to? Historically, speech covers both spoken and written words. In today's world, speech includes email, texting, messaging, and even emoji use. It can also include nonverbal communication such as facial expressions and body language.

Buddha describes four primary abstentions in the realm of right speech. The first is to abstain from false speech or lying; its corollary is to tell the truth. False speech is defined as the intent to knowingly deceive others. It includes any attempts to manipulate others for a certain gain. It also includes exaggerating (for example, how long it took to get somewhere or how much money you make). It does not include speaking something false with a wholehearted belief that it is true. Even so, Buddha advises that if one does not know, one should say, "I don't know."

The second is to abstain from slanderous or divisive speech that intends to cause disagreement between people. Divisive speech, rooted in hate and aversion, is a serious transgression with great unwholesome kamma. Instead, Buddha encourages speech that unites others and promotes harmony.

The third is to abstain from harsh or abusive speech. This refers to any speech spoken in anger and intended to cause harm to the listener. Harsh speech includes insulting, scolding, shaming, and mocking. Its correlated encouragement is to speak gently, kindly, and lovingly, even when it requires great patience.

The fourth is to abstain from idle chatter, or pointless conversation that lacks wholesome direction. This includes gossip, distracting entertainment, and mindless prattle. By committing to these four abstentions, we can refrain from unwholesome and harmful speech.

## Lessons from Right Speech

How might we bridge the gap between knowing the four abstentions for wise speech and actually living by them in daily life? Buddha offers some simple guidelines for how to approach this.

Right speech must be true, useful, kind, and timely. For communication to be considered right speech, it must meet all four of these criteria. This means speech could be true, useful, and kind, but if the timing is not right, it is not right speech! But what makes speech timely? One way we might interpret the timeliness of right speech is considering whether the hearer is ready to receive the message being shared.

Let's say a close friend of ours is having a conflict in their romantic relationship and comes to us about it. We may feel that we have the perfect solution to their woes. Our response could be based in truths we have observed for ourselves, said in a kind, inoffensive way, and be truly useful to our friend. But what if our friend is distraught and primarily in need of emotional support in this moment? Or what if they are in a state of anger and defensiveness and not open to receiving advice? No matter how perfect our solution, if our friend is not ready to receive it, it is *not* right speech.

One way we might apply such an approach to assessing our speech is to regularly pause and check in with ourselves: "Is what I'm about to say true? Is it kind? Is it useful? Is it in good timing?" If the answer to all of these questions is "yes," we can proceed. If not, we might want to consider withholding our speech and examining our views and intentions.

Another way to incorporate right speech into our daily lives is to make a regular commitment to the five precepts, or rules of training, that comprise the basic code of ethics for Buddhist lay practitioners (people who are not monks or nuns). These are explored in more detail in the chapter on right action (page 73). Reflecting on, committing to, and even chanting these precepts can help cultivate a sense of ethical integrity and mindfulness toward our speech and actions.

# CHAPTER II

# Sammā-kammanta
## (Right Action)

In this chapter, we will explore the meaning of right action, including the lessons we can draw from it. We'll also investigate options to modify some aspects of right action for our contemporary and modern ways of existing.

## What Is Right Action?

The second ethical training of the sīla group is right action. Actions are deeds performed with the body. They include interacting directly with other living beings in ways outside of speech such as hugging, harming, and sexual intimacy. Actions also include our interactions with non-sentient objects like purchasing, taking, and using items.

As with right speech, Buddha names a series of abstentions that constitute right action. The first is abstaining from taking life from any sentient being. Yes, even bugs! This abstention also includes refraining from harming or torturing living beings without killing them. The understanding here is that all living beings love life and seek happiness while fearing death and experiencing aversion to pain. We are encouraged to feel sympathy and compassion for all beings and can also frame the wholesome opposite of this abstention as "support all forms of life."

The second abstention that constitutes wise action is abstaining from taking what is not given. This essentially comes down to not stealing, but it also includes refraining from fraud and cheating, all actions based in the unwholesome root of greed. It does not include taking that which does not have an owner. The wholesome opposites of this abstention are to practice gratitude and generosity.

The third abstention is refraining from sexual misconduct. For monastics (monks and nuns) this guideline means practicing celibacy. As lay practitioners, we may choose to practice celibacy for periods of time, but we can also interpret this guideline as referring to misconduct only and not sexual activity generally.

Buddha defines sexual misconduct in terms of prohibited sexual partners, but this does not necessarily translate well to today's world. One way we might interpret the abstention from sexual misconduct is with a focus on consent of all parties involved in a sexual interaction. This means that sexual relations with individuals under the age of consent is considered sexual misconduct, as well as with anyone under the influence of intoxicants and unable to give sound consent.

This interpretation also makes space for evolving social norms. In today's world, ethical non-monogamy is gaining in popularity, and marriage does not necessarily prohibit sexual partners outside of marriage. In the context of a consent interpretation, extramarital sexual relations are not considered sexual misconduct if everyone consents. That said, if one or more parties involved in the sexual relationship are not aware, do not give their consent, or have been persuaded or coerced into giving consent, the relationship is considered sexual misconduct by those engaging in sexual activity.

Overall, when navigating sexual relations, we should keep in mind the other ethical abstentions: we should refrain from deceit, refrain from speech meant to manipulate others for one's own sexual benefit, and never engage in forced or violent sexual acts. In this way, we can avoid sexual misconduct.

We can also practice bringing mindfulness to compulsive sexual energy. Like most things, sex can become addictive and lead to further taṇhā for ourselves. The intention of wise actions around sexual activity is to prevent sexual relations that are harmful, and this applies to ourselves as well as others. By bringing awareness to how we use and engage sexual energy, we can promote more harmony and less suffering in the realm of intimacy.

## Lessons from Right Action

The abstentions for right action are expanded upon in the five precepts, the set of training guidelines that practitioners often commit to regularly. These precepts are to abstain from killing and harming, to abstain from stealing, to abstain from sexual misconduct, to abstain from false speech, and to abstain from intoxicants. In this way, the five precepts incorporate the three abstentions of right action, right speech, and an additional guideline: to abstain from intoxicants.

The guideline about abstaining from intoxicants refers to the use of alcohol and drugs. For monastics, this means abstaining completely from the use of intoxicants; for lay practitioners, this can mean refraining from unskillful use of intoxicants.

The intention here is to keep the mind clear and capable of skillful discernment, to maintain right view and right intention, and to be able to tell what is the cause of suffering and what is not.

When we partake in unskillful quantities of alcohol and other recreational drugs, the mind can become foggy and unable to clearly see what will and will not lead to further dukkha. We also run the risk of creating unwholesome kamma of addiction to these substances, such that we are more likely to partake of them again in the future. However, we should note that this aspect of right action does not include psychiatric and other medically necessary prescription medicines. This precept simply encourages us to practice mindfulness and skillful use of intoxicants, should we choose to use them.

Overall, the five precepts are a useful tool for remembering and practicing right speech and right action in daily life. One practice we might consider is writing out our own version of the precepts based on our specific lifestyle and needs. This allows us to make adjustments based on what is reasonable and reachable for us at this time, and also to use language that resonates with us. We can then practice taking or recommitting to our custom precepts on a weekly basis.

Some precept adjustments we might consider:

**Abstain from killing and harming:** If we need animal protein for medical reasons, we might allow limited meat consumption or animal supplements. If our home is overrun with a destructive or disease-carrying pest, we might make an exception for ethical, minimally harming pest management.

**Abstain from taking that which is not ours:** We might expand this precept by also committing to deliberate gratitude and generosity. We might keep a gratitude journal or find a way to practice *dāna*, or generosity, daily.

**Abstain from sexual misconduct:** In addition to consent, we might develop our own guidelines for individuals who are and are not ethical choices for sexual partners for us based on relationship statuses, history, context, and peoples' capacities. We also might commit to bringing mindfulness to our sexual and romantic energy when interacting with our sexual partners.

**Abstain from intoxicants:** Some intoxicants that are considered recreational drugs are also considered medicinal when used intentionally. We might write a precept that allows for such mindful and intentional use.

# CHAPTER 12

# Sammā-ajiva
## (Right Livelihood)

In this chapter, we will explore the meaning of right livelihood, including the lessons we can draw from it.

## What Is Right Livelihood?

The third and final aspect of the moral discipline group of the Path
is *sammā-ajiva* or right livelihood. Right livelihood refers to the way
we earn a living here in samsāra. Also included in right livelihood is
the manner by which we engage in our work.

Buddha provides four primary guidelines for how we should
earn an ethical living. First, the method by which we earn wealth
should be legal. Second, it should be peaceful and without violence. Third, we should only acquire wealth honestly and without
deceit. Finally, we must only acquire wealth in a way that does not
involve harm and suffering to other living beings.

These guidelines may seem difficult to abide by in today's world.
For example, the first guideline means under-the-table work is not
right livelihood. The second guideline suggests that any jobs within
or supporting the military or police force cannot be considered right
livelihood, since they involve violence. The third guideline about not

acquiring wealth through deceit doesn't align with many commonly accepted business and government practices widely used today.

On top of all that, Buddha also names five additional types of livelihood that should be avoided because participating in them strengthens systems that do further harm in vast ways on a larger scale:

- Dealing in weapons
- Dealing in living beings (human trafficking and slave trade, sex work, and raising animals for slaughter)
- Meat production and butchery
- Poisons
- Intoxicants

And, of course, any occupation that violates right speech or right action can also not be considered right livelihood.

How can one possibly find supportive work that meets these criteria? Are we all doomed to be jobless?

Harmful industries driven by the accumulation of wealth have grown more massive, lucrative, and global since the Buddha's times. It is significantly more challenging to make a living that is not tied up in any of these industries today. We might take this teaching lightly then, as an invitation for reflection and consideration about the nature of our work and how we perform it.

For example, we might consider *how* we engage our work. If our only work option is to raise animals for slaughter, can we advocate for the ethical treatment of the animals? If we work as a butcher, can we source our products from ethical farms rather than factory farms? If we work in a liquor store, can we make sure to never sell to someone underage nor to individuals who are intoxicated beyond functioning?

And what if our sector of work does feel like right livelihood? Are we "off the hook" for this practice? Well, in addition to bringing the five precepts to our time at work, we can also practice right livelihood by working diligently and with integrity. We can do our best to focus when we are on the clock, and take time away from work when we need it. In this way, we can practice right livelihood in an ongoing way, no matter our industry.

## Lessons from Right Livelihood

Even though we exist in a globalized capitalist system and don't always have much control in the type of work available to us, we can apply the teaching on sammā-ajiva by reflecting on the work we do find ourselves in. We might also consider our purchasing and consumer decisions as an extended aspect of right livelihood, taking into account the companies we choose to buy from. In addition to refraining from working for harmful industries as much as possible, we can also do our best to refrain from supporting harmful industries in this way. Again, this is far more difficult in today's economy, so we should not take such a suggestion as an absolute. Furthermore, shopping ethically is usually a choice that can only be made by a few privileged individuals capable of paying more for their necessities. However, we can simply choose to bring mindfulness to the industries that source our clothing, food, toiletries, and technology, and when an option occasionally arises to support an ethical purchasing choice within our means, we can take it when our budgets allow.

Similarly, sammā-ajiva invites us to reflect on our relationship to the material world in general. What is our relationship to money? To shopping? To consumerism? Buddha advises that we not possess more than is necessary. As lay practitioners, this doesn't mean we need to let go of every object that might be considered indulgent, but rather to reflect on how we interact with such objects and our experiences with them.

Do we feel a sense of intense clinging or even addiction to making money or buying things? What does it feel like in the body when we place an online order? Or is there anxiety and fear around money, and thus a clinging to the wealth that we do have? Do work, money, or shopping feel like a distraction from spiritual practice? How do our ethical commitments show up in these realms? By asking ourselves these questions, we can approach our livelihood and spending from a more grounded and intentional place.

# CHAPTER 13

# Sammā-vayama
## (Right Effort)

In this chapter, we will explore the meaning of right effort, including the lessons we can draw from it.

## What Is Right Effort?

The remaining three factors on the Path form the concentration or samādhi group. They are right effort, right mindfulness, and right concentration. Each of these factors is a form of direct mental training with the ultimate goal of achieving sustained concentration. A still, focused mind is considered necessary for the emergence of wisdom that ultimately liberates us from suffering.

The first of the concentration group is sammā-vayama or right effort. We can think of effort as taking up spiritual practice with determination, exertion, and perseverance. We can also consider it to be the conscious joining of intention with action.

The spiritual path requires a significant amount of energy and commitment; it is literally the work of transforming the mind. We start with the mind as we find it when we embark on the Path: likely riddled with confusion, delusion, anger, and attachment. We then apply relentless wholesome energy, fueled by right view and intention, to the mind's purification and awakening. This is right effort.

We can think of right effort in terms of our meditation practice in general, as we might bring effort to learning a musical instrument or a new language. However, Buddha also provides four specific exertions to apply right effort toward. They are:

1. To prevent unwholesome states from arising

2. To abandon unwholesome states that have arisen

3. To cultivate wholesome states that have not arisen

4. To maintain and perfect wholesome states that have arisen

What is an unwholesome state? We can think of them as the mind-states, thoughts, and emotions associated with the three poisons of greed, aversion, and delusion. They are unwholesome because they ultimately lead to more dukkha. Such states could include hatred, envy, arrogance, and confusion.

In meditation, the three poisons can be expanded into five discrete mental factors that impede our practice. They are referred to as the five hindrances. The five hindrances are:

- Sense desire

- Ill will

- Sloth and torpor (dullness and drowsiness)

- Restlessness and worry

- Doubt

Before we take on an antagonistic stance to these hindrances, we might consider that these are perfectly natural human states that often indicate a valid need we have. They just so happen to become obstacles in our meditation practice and therefore require our right effort. Let us approach them kindly and with curiosity.

It might be helpful to understand and approach the hindrances as some of the seven dwarves from the fairy tale "Snow White," for example:

1. Sense desire as Sneezy: distracted by and reactive to the external world

2. Ill will as Grumpy: angry and irritable

3. Sloth and torpor as Sleepy: drowsy, heavy, and constantly falling asleep

4. Restlessness and worry as Bashful: self-conscious, anxious, excited, and embarrassed

5. Doubt as Doc: overly analytical, distrustful, and slightly conceited

As we encounter these hindrances in meditation practice and apply right effort to prevent and abandon them, we might picture these precious characters to bring a gentle playfulness to our practice.

If these are unwholesome states, then wholesome states can simply be considered mental states, thoughts, and emotions without the presence of the three poisons or the five hindrances. We can strive to interact with unwholesome and wholesome states appropriately using right effort as we work to transform the mind in our practice.

# Lessons from Right Effort

The first two exertions instruct us to apply right effort to prevent and abandon unwholesome states such as the five hindrances. How might we do that?

The first exertion, the endeavor to restrain, involves applying effort to keep from tumbling into the hindrances. One way we can do this is by bringing mindfulness to our senses. The hindrances often arise in response to sensory information: a craving for the lovely smell of cookies, ill will or aversion toward the sound of traffic, sloth and torpor if the body feels tired, etc. Mindfulness of the senses keeps us focused on what is being sensed *before* that information can spiral into evaluations or judgments about the experience, which introduce the hindrances. We might then think of this endeavor as the practice of experiencing things exactly as they are.

That said, even with vigilant sense-mindfulness, the hindrances still arise at times. That's why the second exertion, the endeavor to abandon, instructs us to work skillfully with the hindrances when they arise in practice. Fortunately for us, each of the five hindrances have an antidote: a mental factor that counteract its effects. Remembering that, we can practice right effort by identifying hindrances as they arise in practice, and then applying their antidotes as needed.

**Sense desire** represents greed and craving; we can notice this hindrance whenever we find ourselves wanting something in our meditation: a snack, a massage, to readjust or move the body, or to get up and be finished with meditating! When we notice sense desire arising, we can reflect on impermanence. The objects of our desire are temporary, as is our wanting. Holding this awareness, we may see the sense desire dissipate.

**Ill will** represents aversion; we can notice it when we find ourselves pushing anything away in meditation: bothered by a feeling of pain in our legs, startling at a sudden unexpected sound, or frustrated by a social struggle. The antidotes for ill will are loving-kindness and compassion practice. Instructions for these brahma-viharas are in chapter 17 (page 121).

**Sloth and torpor** are a form of delusion; it is present when we feel lazy, tired, fatigued, numb, or apathetic. To work skillfully with this hindrance, we should stir up the energy to wake up the body. We might take a break from seated meditation practice to exercise or go for a walk, get a cup of tea, or even take a power nap.

**Restlessness and worry** are also a form of delusion; we might see it arise as feeling anxious, tense, and excited, or a racing mind. The antidote is to take steps to calm the body. We might practice mindfulness of breathing, listen to our heartbeat, or spend time in nature. We can also release pent-up energy through exercise.

**Doubt** is the third form of delusion and can appear as a lack of confidence in the teachings or our practice. Its antidote is to investigate: to ask questions and study the teachings until more clarity and confidence arises.

As an alternative to these antidotes, right effort can also be applied by repeatedly redirecting our attention away from a hindrance that is arising, without repressing it. For example, if we find that we get lost in planning thoughts during meditation practice, then we can redirect our mind back to the present moment as soon as we notice. We can also look at the hindrance head-on and investigate its source. We might ask ourselves, are we tired because we are getting sick and need to rest? Are we anxious because we have a lot of work responsibilities right now? Hindrances can arise when we have a need that is not being met; in those cases, we should work to meet that need.

The third and fourth exertions are about applying right effort to wholesome states. The focus here is on cultivating states such as right view, right intention, the brahma-viharas, and the seven enlightenment factors, which are:

| 1. Mindfulness | 5. Tranquility or calm |
|---|---|
| 2. Investigation | 6. Concentration |
| 3. Effort or energy | 7. Equanimity |
| 4. Joy or rapture | |

Guided meditations for cultivating these states can be a great approach.

Finally, the endeavor to maintain is about guarding and sustaining these wholesome states for the sake of liberation. This is the ultimate goal of right effort and is further developed through right mindfulness and right concentration.

# CHAPTER 14

# Sammā-sati
## (Right Mindfulness)

In this chapter, we will explore the meaning of right mindfulness, including the lessons we can draw from it.

## What Is Right Mindfulness?

Right effort as applied to wholesome and unwholesome states in meditation requires the next factor of the Path, *sammā-sati*, or right mindfulness. Mindfulness can be defined as nonjudgmental awareness of the present moment. It can be applied to every moment of every day and also cultivated in formal meditation practice.

Mindfulness has gained traction and popularity in recent years as a method for increasing productivity, sharpening focus, and promoting well-being. However, *sati* as the Buddha taught it is not complete without a firm grounding in right view, right intention, and ethics. Committed to the liberation from suffering and intent on renunciation, goodwill, and harmlessness, we practice mindfulness to calm the mind and see things as they really are.

Sati is about touching into the ultimate nature of reality. By coming into the present moment and experiencing it exactly as it is, with nonjudgmental awareness, we begin to awaken. We should recall that enlightenment is our true nature. Buddha-nature is within us and is naturally revealed as we clear away the obstacles blocking and distorting our view of reality.

Buddha suggests four primary contemplations toward which to direct our mindfulness practice. They are:

1. The body

2. *Vedanā* (feelings)

3. States of mind

4. *Dhammas* (phenomena)

Together these are referred to as the *four foundations of mindfulness*, and sometimes called the direct path to realization. By pointing our nonjudgmental, present-moment awareness to these four realms, we pave the way for liberation.

Mindfulness of the body usually begins with mindfulness of breathing or *ānāpānasati*, but it can also include the heartbeat or our body position. Mindfulness of feeling or vedanā refers to the sense experience of an object and the valence of an experience: whether it is pleasant, painful, or neutral. States of mind refer to the various mental processes or events that arise, including thoughts, desires, and emotions. Mindfulness of phenomena, also called dhammas, refers to awareness of the totality of our experience unfolding in an interdependent, ongoing manner.

An important aspect of mindfulness is that we refrain from judgments and interpretations of our experience. When practicing this does not mean that judgments do not arise, but that we interact with them skillfully. Let's say a judgmental thought arises while we are meditating such as "I suck at this." We can notice the thought kindly, perhaps give it a label or name such as "judgment," and then gently redirect the attention back to the contemplation.

By engaging with mindfulness, we choose to step back from the complex framework that the mind has constructed and tries to insert our experience into. We witness the present moment, breaking down each interpretation, association, and narrative that arises until all that is left is the bare experience. In this way, we divest from the storied version of experience that our minds construct and learn to pay attention to the raw information of the four contemplations, moment after moment.

All this said, this process does not have to mean that we invalidate or repress the mind's constructed version of experience. As we become aware of such constructions, we can bring a heart of compassion and perhaps even gratitude that the mind has gone to such great lengths to help us survive. For this reason, we might also choose to think of sati as "heartfulness."

## Lessons from Right Mindfulness

Buddha provides specific instructions for how to practice mindfulness meditation in a formal practice approach through the four foundations of mindfulness. These instructions have been examined and analyzed extensively by great Buddhist scholars and are worthy of much time and attention. However, we can also apply sammā-sati to daily life by checking in with our experience throughout the day.

In any given moment during the day, we might take a pause and try out a five-factor check-in. This integrated practice can be useful when we notice that we are especially caught up in thoughts or distraction and would benefit from grounding in the present moment. The five factors we can check in with are the external environment, the body, emotions, thoughts, and the Heartspace or awareness itself.

As we take a pause and begin a check in, we might start with our external environment. Looking around us, we can take in the shapes and colors of the objects in the room or outdoors. In an enclosed area, we might also locate the exit, as this can help calm an overactive nervous system, by confirming that there is a way to escape the current situation if the need were to arise. We might also focus on any sounds or smells that are present.

Moving on to the body, which relates to the first foundation of mindfulness, we can ask ourselves how the body feels. Do we feel full or hungry? Hot or cold? Is the body energized, fatigued, stiff, tense, painful, at ease? What bodily sensations do we observe?

The third factor, emotions, corresponds to the emotion aspect of the "states of mind" foundation of mindfulness. We might check in with our emotions by simply labeling them: excited, sad, angry, overwhelmed, confused, worried, content. The practice here is not to analyze the emotions, but simply to bring mindful awareness to what is present.

The fourth factor, thoughts, corresponds to the cognitive aspects of the "states of mind" foundation of mindfulness. Similar to our check-ins with the body and emotions, we can ask ourselves what thoughts are present. What kind of mental activity is most dominant in our experience? We might once again try labeling them: planning, daydreaming, remembering, analyzing, fantasizing. Again, we need not follow the trains of thought to their conclusions, but just watch them arise, give them a label, and let them fall away again.

The final factor we might check in on is our awareness itself, which loosely corresponds to the fourth foundation of mindfulness. We might do this by placing a hand on the heart and spending a moment or two concentrating on the Heartspace. We might also turn our focus inward and be with our stillness within for a moment. This factor allows us to return to our spacious awareness regardless of all that we observed in the four other factors.

To each of these factors we offer nonjudgmental present-moment awareness, acknowledging the environment, body sensations, emotions, thoughts, and quality of observing arising without any attempt to alter them. We might also label them as pleasant, painful, or neutral, and observe how they arise and fall away. In this way, we bring the feelings foundation of mindfulness to the check-in. This need not be a lengthy practice, but can be a quick tool to bring sammā-sati to spare moments throughout the day.

And so, through both formal mindfulness meditation and integrated sati practices throughout the day, we incorporate sammā-sati into our spiritual path.

# CHAPTER 15

# Sammā-samādhi
## (Right Concentration)

In this chapter, we will explore the meaning of right concentration, including the lessons we can draw from it, before examining meditation practice as another way to deepen right concentration. The chapter will close with a useful anecdote to ground these concepts and a journaling practice dedicated to the Noble Eightfold Path.

## What Is Right Concentration?

The final aspect of the Noble Eightfold Path is *sammā-samādhi* or right concentration. Concentration can be defined as wholesome one-pointedness of the mind and absorption with the meditative object. It usually refers specifically to formal meditation practice.

Like right mindfulness and effort, right concentration as taught by the Buddha is only complete when grounded in right view, intention, and moral discipline. It is fueled by the aid of right effort and right mindfulness. Effort provides the energy demanded of the task of focusing, while mindfulness stabilizes awareness and provides corrections to keep the mind steadied. Mindfulness can also protect the mind from the five hindrances that threaten to push concentration off course. But what is it that the mind concentrates on?

In formal practice, we cultivate concentration by training with a meditation object or anchor. A meditation object is a neutral, steady, reliable phenomenon that is always present for us to observe and focus on for the purposes of training the mind. The breath is the most common meditation object. However, for trauma survivors the breath can be far from neutral and actually re-traumatizing to focus on. Other suitable meditation objects to consider are the heartbeat; the sensations where the body makes contact with the cushion, floor, or chair; and sound or auditory information. Whatever object feels neutral and reliable to us can serve as an appropriate anchor for concentration practice.

In addition to a basic go-to meditation object such as the breath, heartbeat, physical sensations, or sounds, we can also cultivate concentration by meditating on certain states and truths described by the Buddha. The four brahma-viharas or divine abodes (page 121) are often used as meditation objects, as are the triple gem of Buddha (teacher), Sangha (community), and Dharma (teachings). Such approaches to concentration can awaken love, compassion, joy, equanimity, devotion, and faith from within the concentrative state.

It is generally thought that concentration training leads to eight jhānas or high meditative states characterized by profound equanimity and the withdrawal of the mind from the senses. The jhānas are often considered some of the most esoteric and poorly understood of the Buddha's teachings, so much of what we know about these states of consciousness is up for debate.

That said, there are thought to be five jhāna factors or factors of absorption that aid the practitioner in achieving one-pointed concentration on the meditation object by overcoming the five hindrances. The five jhāna factors are:

1. Initial application of the mind

2. Sustained application of the mind

3. Rapture

4. Happiness

5. One-pointedness

Initial application of the mind is about willing the mind toward the object of meditation. It might look like directing and redirecting the mind to its meditation object again and again; this factor opposes the hindrance of sloth and torpor. Sustained application of the mind then anchors the mind on the object alone, keeping it there with unbroken continuity; it opposes doubt. These first two factors have also been translated to "thinking" and "examining."

The third jhāna factor, rapture, is an arising of interest in the meditation object and delighting in focusing on it; it opposes aversion. Happiness, the fourth factor, is a feeling of pleasure or contentment with the successful concentration; it opposes restlessness and worry. The final factor is one-pointedness and refers to the unwavering unification of the mind with the meditation object; it opposes sense desire.

As we develop right concentration through meditation practice, these five factors arise and aid us on our journey to absorption. Rapture and happiness in particular are powerful aspects of concentration practice that encourage us to cultivate focus. In this way, we come to know reality exactly as it is, one meditation object at a time.

# Lessons from Right Concentration

Sammā-samādhi shows us that ultimately to engage with the Noble Eightfold Path, we must have some sort of meditation practice. Most of the factors of the Path can be cultivated in daily life; while we can practice concentration to some degree while going about our day, true one-pointed absorption can really only be cultivated while directing all efforts toward meditation.

So, how might we go about starting a meditation practice? As we might already know from practicing other skills such as a musical instrument or a new language, consistency is key. In starting a meditation practice, we must find an approach that feels accessible and even enticing to us. Meditation should be an interesting and nourishing endeavor, not a chore we check off a to-do list. So, as we approach the task of forming a regular practice, we should tread lightly and err on the side of ease.

Some variables we might consider in approaching a practice are:

- Type of meditation to practice
- Bodily posture to take for practice
- Length of a practice period
- Choosing a teacher and sangha

In selecting our initial type of meditation, we might benefit from a simple approach such as mindfulness of breathing, breath-counting, or mindfulness-of-senses. However, we can also choose a type of meditation that feels most relevant or resonant in the heart. Perhaps we feel that compassion is readily accessible to us because of suffering we have witnessed or experienced. In that case, a karuṇā practice may be a skillful starting place.

We also may choose to begin with a guided meditation found on Dharma Seed, YouTube, InsightTimer, HeadSpace, or a dharma text; see the Resources section (page 134) for more information. We can listen to a teacher's guidance and practice the meditation in real time according to their instructions. Alternatively, we can read meditation instructions from a book, taking one line at a time and sitting with the instructions in-between.

Before diving in too deep to meditation, we will also want to examine our bodily posture. Primarily we should care for our body's ability and comfort. If the body has any disabilities or constraints that make cross-legged sitting uncomfortable, painful, or impossible, we should not attempt to do so. Buddha does not praise cross-legged meditation above any other bodily postures. We can try meditating in a chair, lying down, standing upright, or walking. Most important, we should aim to keep our backs straight, shoulders and face relaxed, mouth closed, and heart open. In this way, we maintain an alert but relaxed posture for practice.

In figuring out how long to meditate in the beginning, we may again want to err on the side of ease. We can begin with as little as one to two minutes of meditation practice at a time—yes, one to two minutes only! Starting small is beneficial because it builds our confidence and excitement about the practice, helps us carefully cultivate habits in our posture and approach, and encourages us to meditate more often. From there we can add minutes of meditation on a schedule that feels good for us. One goal we might consider is to work up to a twenty-minute meditation one or two times per day, but there are many variations of this goal that are also effective for lay practitioners.

Finally, we may choose to take on a teacher and a sangha (dharma community). We can look into the three major schools of Buddhism (*theravāda, mahāyāna, vajrayāna*), and see what communities are near us. We might listen to a couple of dharma talks online or drop in to a class or group meeting. We can bring mindfulness to these experiences and see which groups and teachers resonate with us. At one point, Buddha says that the sangha—the community—is the whole of the Path. It is essential that we surround ourselves with other practitioners to encourage our spiritual growth along the Noble Eightfold Path.

# Being Mindful of Morals

Imagine an ordinary workday: you wake up, do your morning routine, go to work, interact with coworkers and maybe a boss, eat a meal, maybe do some care for the body, spend time with family, roommates, a pet, or on your own, wind down, and go to sleep.

Throughout such a day, you make countless choices about what you say, how you behave, and how you work to make ends meet. But what if you brought sammā-sati—right mindfulness—to your ethical decisions throughout such a regular day?

Starting with your morning routine, think about what you eat and drink and how you care for yourself as you're waking up. Do you have any morning interactions? Which of your actions and words tend to be wholesome and kind to yourself and others? Which might lead to more suffering?

Imagine your commute to work. Do you drive? Carpool? Bus? Bike? With whom do you interact along the way? What is the nature of those interactions? Remember, sammā-sati is about *nonjudgmental* awareness. Do not *judge* your actions as right or wrong; simply see them exactly as they are and feel what it is like to observe their relationship to suffering.

You get to work. Maybe you begin interacting with customers or coworkers right away, or maybe you work from home or in a cubicle on your own. Do you talk with anyone? What do you say? What are the intentions behind your words? What is the effect of your words? Bring mindfulness to these interactions as you reflect on them. Which are wholesome? Which are less wholesome?

And now, how are you making money? What are you doing to earn that paycheck? What are the effects of your occupation? Your company? Your industry? How does your work lead to suffering, and how does it lead to liberation from suffering? Bring mindfulness to your body, emotions, and thoughts as you contemplate these. Allow nonjudgmental awareness to pervade your reflections.

At last, you get home from work. How do you unwind? What do you eat, drink, watch, or read? Do you purchase anything, like dinner, groceries, or other shopping? If so, how do you make your purchasing decisions? Examine how these choices are wholesome and unwholesome, again bringing nonjudgmental awareness to the true nature of these things. Do not condemn yourself for any unwholesome actions; just bring mindfulness to what it feels like.

As the evening wears on, you begin to settle down. How do you process your day? How do you prepare your body and mind for rest? Do you spend time with people or animals you live with, and if so, what are the nature of those interactions? Do you tend to be grumpy and tired from a long day of work? How do you tend to the needs of yourself and others?

The Noble Eightfold Path can be applied to any day in this way. The factor of sammā-sati is not separate from the moral discipline group, which is based in right view and right intention. Come back to this anecdote any time you want to practice applying the Path to the day-to-day.

# MY EIGHTFOLD PATH

This is a contemplative journaling exercise to reflect on how the Noble Eightfold Path fits into your life. As you engage in this exercise, write freely about whatever comes to mind first. Refrain from editing or censoring what comes up for you. You can revisit this practice over time as your life circumstances change and your practice progresses.

Start with a large piece of paper. Draw a circle that fills the entire page, and divide the circle into eight sections. Starting at the top right, label each section with the eight aspects of the Path.

In the right view section, write down what you believe. What is your perspective about how the universe works? What is the nature of phenomena? Do not try to adhere to a Buddhist belief system; write what your heart believes to be true in this moment.

In the right intention section, write whatever intentions are present in your heart now.

In the right speech, action, and livelihood sections, write down some guidelines you hold for yourself in each of these realms.

In right effort, write down the endeavors that mean most to you and that you are actively striving toward.

In right mindfulness, jot down the bodily sensations, emotions, and mental activity that you are aware of in this moment.

In right concentration, write the name of a single meditation object. Set down your pen and focus on your selected meditation object for five minutes or more.

# PART IV

# OTHER BUDDHIST TEACHINGS

## — Wisdom Gained —

In this section, we will explore two additional Buddhist teachings that may not fit as neatly into the previous lists but are still useful aspects of starting a Buddhist practice: the five spiritual faculties (or powers) and the four brahma-viharas. Taken together, these two sets of inner states can be cultivated within us and used as powerful signs of progress along the Path. The five spiritual faculties can be thought of as mental states and the four brahma-viharas can be thought of as heart states.

# CHAPTER 16

# Pancha Bala/Indriya
## (The Five Spiritual Faculties or Powers)

In this chapter, we will explore the meaning of the five spiritual faculties, including the lessons we can draw from them, and how we can think about them in more precise detail.

## What are the Five Spiritual Faculties?

The five spiritual faculties (*pancha indriya*) are faith, effort, mindfulness, concentration, and wisdom, and are also sometimes called the five cardinal virtues. Buddha describes them as one and the same as the five powers (*pancha balas*) when cultivated to their potential. Together, these mirrored sets of five states are two of the seven sets of wholesome qualities conducive to awakening, along with other sets we have explored in the earlier chapters, including the four foundations of mindfulness, the four exertions, and the Noble Eightfold Path.

We can think of these five faculties as some of the foremost positive qualities of the enlightened mind. In following the instructions of the Eightfold Path, we can look to the five spiritual faculties as encouraging indicators of our progress. They can also serve as objects of contemplation and cultivation. As these states grow in the mind, they become protective factors against the three poisons, transforming them into fuel for further awakening.

The order of the cultivation of these states, while not absolute, is relevant as each state leads to the next. Faith produces energy that naturally brings forth effort. In a state of abundant effort, mindfulness arises with ease. Greater mindfulness leads to a more steadied, concentrated mind, and wisdom of the true nature of reality emerges from the still, concentrated mind.

## Saddhā (Faith)

The first spiritual faculty is *saddhā* or faith. We can think of saddhā as trust and confidence in the dharma and awakening. Saddhā also composes right view: a thorough understanding of and confidence in karma, rebirth, the Four Noble Truths, and the Three Marks of Existence.

Sometimes faith can be a tricky word for people who may have associations with the term from a Christian tradition. In the Buddhist context, we can think of faith as provisional: we only need to be curious or trusting enough to try a teaching out for ourselves. We might read about compassion practice, feel some sense of resonance within, and then take that leap of faith to actually try sitting and meditating on compassion. Such an investment of our time and energy is saddhā.

We are never expected to take teachings on blind faith, and trust is built up over time through direct personal experience. So as we begin practice, we only need enough trust to explore the teachings openly. From such an initial exploration, confidence grows and eventually forms a sense of conviction about the Path and our practice. Over time, we can begin to trust the possibility of liberation for ourselves and all beings. This experience of saddhā is said to help block the five hindrances and bring about serenity as we continue on the Path.

## Viriya (Effort)

The second spiritual faculty is *viriya* or effort. It is also sometimes translated as vigor or energy. If it sounds familiar, it's not altogether distinct from right effort, the sixth factor on the Eightfold Path. We can think of viriya as the energy we bring forth to initiate and continue engaging in our meditation and spiritual practice. This can mean making ethical commitments by taking our precepts each week, reading dharma texts, listening to dharma talks regularly to cultivate right view and intention, and showing up for meditation practice.

Like the right effort stage on the Path, we can also consider viriya in the context of the four exertions: to prevent and abandon unwholesome states, and to cultivate and maintain wholesome states. Working skillfully with the hindrances as they arise is powerful viriya cultivation, as are wholesome contemplations like the four foundations of mindfulness. Essentially, by bringing earnest commitment to working skillfully in a mindfulness meditation practice, we are using and growing our viriya muscle.

Viriya arises out of faith because it is our initial curiosity about the teachings, and then our growing confidence in them, that leads us to practice. There is a natural arising and flow of energy toward practice from the state of saddha, and so the faculties build one another.

## Sati (Mindfulness)

The third spiritual faculty is sati, or mindfulness, and mirrors one of the stages of the Path. Recall that mindfulness can be defined as nonjudgmental awareness of the present moment.

Sati arises when we direct viriya toward practices such as contemplations on the four foundations of mindfulness. By bringing our fullest, least-obstructed attention to the spheres of the body, feeling, mind-states, and phenomena, we can carefully cultivate and experience sati.

Sati is said to be the only factor of the mind that we can never have too much of, as it does not push us toward overexcitement nor laziness as the other faculties can. In this way, we can think of mindfulness as a core practice that we can return to again and again, no matter our emotional or mental capacities in any given moment. It requires minimal discernment and is easily cultivated whether on the cushion in formal practice or throughout the day.

One additional way we might think about mindfulness is in terms of remembering. A practice in mindfulness can be thought of as repeatedly recalling the intention to pay attention, to let go of judgment, and to allow our experience to arise exactly as it is. When we slip out of sati, we are simply forgetting this intention. As we cultivate sati, we learn to remember more often.

## Samādhi (Concentration)

Like the final factor on the Noble Eightfold Path, the fourth spiritual faculty is samādhi or concentration. Recall that concentration refers to cultivating one-pointed attention and working with the jhāna states in formal meditation practice. Concentration arises naturally when we bring forth effort toward mindfulness in formal practice, and we cultivate it by directing attention toward meditation objects, including wholesome states.

So often in our daily life, the mind is scattered with countless different lines of thinking, realms of awareness, and mental activity. We often find such chaos when we enter into formal meditation practice as well. Meditations focused on concentration can be thought of as bringing kind discipline to the mind, training it to sit and focus on just one object at a time. In this way, we cultivate concentration by returning to our object of meditation again and again through the application of effort in formal practice.

Over time, we may begin to notice the more frantic aspects of the mind dissipate, and directing the mind to focus on a single object becomes easier. This can also carry over into daily life, and we may observe more calmness and less reactivity as we go about our days. To understand such shifts, we might visualize that as the mind's usually chaotic energies focus in on a single point, spaciousness is created in our awareness to hold all that arises with ease. Our ability to hold space and observe our experience without judging it, without clinging to it, grows.

## Prajñā (Wisdom)

The final spiritual faculty is wisdom or *prajñā*. We can think of wisdom as an embodied, intuitive sense of seeing and understanding how things are. Wisdom can be cultivated, but it also arises on its own through the combination of sati and samādhi.

Wisdom is not merely knowledge or a purely cognitive way of knowing. It is an illuminating, moment-to-moment acknowledgment of reality in its raw form, a way of seeing that opposes delusion and cuts through to the true nature of phenomena.

And what do we know about the true nature of phenomena? We know that existence is marked by impermanence, dissatisfaction, and not-self. We know that dukkha is pervasive and caused by craving but has an end when we follow the Noble Eightfold Path. Seeing these truths clearly in any given moment constitutes wisdom.

Wisdom can also include the ability to hold multiple truths that seem contradictory. For example, in any given moment our awareness might vacillate between the knowing that our unwholesome states such as hatred and anxiety often lead us to further suffering and the knowing that we need to offer them sati: to allow them to be as they are without any judgment. How do we see and acknowledge both the teachings on right effort that tell us to abandon unwholesome states while also bringing the nonjudgment of sati? This is an example of a nuanced, seemingly contradictory set of teachings. We can cultivate prajñā by contemplating such nuanced instructions and practicing knowing the paradoxical truth in an embodied, intuitive way, regardless of whether the cognitive mind can reason its way through.

## Lessons from the Five Spiritual Faculties

We can interact with the five spiritual faculties by thinking about them as virtuous signposts. The spiritual path is about uncovering our true Buddha-nature: the pure, undefiled gem of the enlightened mind. As we progress along the Path, discernment becomes necessary to be able to tell the difference between what is Buddha-nature and what is delusion. We can look to the five spiritual faculties as jewel facets shining in the dark, guiding our way and offering encouragement.

Additionally, the indriya offer us an intuitive progression of mental states that we can bring to our practice. We can use this progression to bring a sense of structure and agency to the at times intimidating task of awakening. As we learn to recognize our own confidence or trust in the teachings and the practice as faith, we know to look out for energy that we can apply as effort to our mindfulness practice. When we feel mindfulness arising with ease, we know that it's a good time to engage in formal concentration practice, where we can hope for wisdom to arise.

As we go about developing these qualities, we should consider that they must be cultivated in a balanced way. Faith taken to an extreme without the balancing influence of wisdom can lead to confidence in the wrong things. Penetrating prajñā about the true nature of things brings balance to overactive saddhā. That said, wisdom without faith can lead to a knowing that is not embodied or acted upon based on ethical trainings. Saddhā and prajñā together result in an appropriate sense of faith based in continuously developing wisdom.

Similarly, an excess of concentration without the balancing effects of viriya can result in sloth and torpor. Too much of the calming effects of concentration make us want to fall asleep! At the same time, an excess of effort without the one-pointed focus of concentration leads to restlessness and worry. Samādhi can balance this tendency with calm and centeredness. Together, viriya and samādhi result in skilled, alert absorption with a meditative object.

Sati is the one faculty that does not require counterbalancing and can also offer usefulness to the other four faculties. Mindfulness allows us to observe right away when the mind becomes too sleepy, too restless, or misled by delusion. In this way, it only serves to broaden awareness and offer us continuous opportunities to correct or realign the mind with our spiritual intentions.

As the spiritual faculties grow and develop together, they eventually take on a protective quality for the mind. There is some threshold of cultivation where these five faculties become controlling faculties that steer us toward liberation. When cultivated to this point, they become the five powers, or pancha balas, and are described in this way because they come to powerfully dominate the whole of our perspective and actions. The five faculties then seem to take on lives of their own as they work to preemptively protect the mind from the three poisons and their manifestation as the five hindrances.

## The Food Faculties

The Buddha taught about the five faculties with regard to spiritual practice, but some of these faculties show up in other areas of our lives as well. We can reflect on how these faculties are natural mental states that we are already aware of in other contexts. From that place of deeper familiarity and understanding, we can cultivate them more skillfully in spiritual practice.

We all have some things in life that we care about and enjoy, things that we already have faith in and put effort toward. Maybe it is spending time with family or friends, playing or watching sports, or engaging with a hobby that we love. Now we'll examine something that every human does and most humans enjoy: eating!

From the time we were born, we began to eat. Since then, we have developed a healthy sense of faith that eating satisfies our hunger, gives us nutrients and energy, and can build connection and community. In this way, we have saddhā in food.

From this trust in the magic of food, most of us are pretty motivated to seek out food that is delicious and nourishing for us. Perhaps we work hard to make enough money to eat out regularly. Or maybe we like to try cooking new recipes. Even if we only do the bare minimum to make sure we get the calories we need, that is still an exertion of effort that comes out of a trust that consuming those calories will do what we want it to do for us. This is viriya.

While many of us may not intentionally bring sati to the eating experience, mindful eating meditations are often considered quite accessible, because when we *do* choose to bring mindfulness to eating, we may find it comes easily; we already have energy around and faith in the experience.

And so, we can reflect on the way that we trust food to satisfy us: what does it feel like to have confidence in food's ability to satisfy our hunger? How does the mind approach food with its learned experience of food's results? We can investigate and spend time with this conviction in the way food serves us so that we can more quickly identify and cultivate similar conviction in the spiritual path.

Reflecting on our tendency to bring effort forth for acquiring and consuming food, we can observe the natural inclination and seemingly effortless energy that pulls us toward the necessary actions. What does it feel like for such energy to arise? We can become familiar with the feeling of viriya in this context so that we can notice with ease when we feel a similar pull to spiritual practice and can take advantage of the opportunity.

Finally, we can practice mindfulness of the eating experience. Directing our attention to the senses, we can focus our awareness on the process of consuming. What do we smell and taste? What is the texture of the food? What aspects of eating do we find pleasant? Unpleasant? Neutral? In this way, we can begin to practice the four foundations of mindfulness in a context that we engage in multiple times every day. From this knowing of sati in the context of eating, we can call it forth more readily from the meditation cushion.

# CHAPTER 17

# Brahma-viharas
## (The Four Immeasurables)

In this chapter, we will explore the meaning of the brahma-viharas, or four immeasurables, including the lessons we can draw from them and how we can explore them further. A useful anecdote at the end will frame how we can think about the four immeasurables in a practical way, and a meditation exercise will serve to bring us closer to our own Heartspace.

## What are the Four Immeasurables?

The brahma-viharas go by many names: the four immeasurables, the divine abodes, the sublime states. They earned the name "immeasurables" because these heart traits can be cultivated to immeasurable, unlimited depths and produce an immeasurable amount of wholesome karma. The brahma-viharas are loving-kindness, compassion, sympathetic joy, and equanimity.

The immeasurable, boundless nature of the brahma-viharas is also indicative of the fact that by their very definitions, these qualities exclude no one. While these aspects of the heart do naturally arise in human life, their nature is to expand beyond just our friends and loved ones. As they are cultivated, they grow beyond the limits we self-impose on our love until the feelings of goodwill and closeness include every living being.

Mettā, or loving-kindness, is often considered the most central of the heart qualities. In fact, we can consider compassion and sympathetic joy to be forms of mettā morphed to meet different contexts. Equanimity, like mindfulness in the five spiritual faculties, provides balance to the other three qualities. Together the brahma-viharas co-create a boundless, awakened heart.

## Mettā (Loving-kindness)

Mettā translates to loving-kindness and includes feelings of goodwill, friendliness, benevolence, and interest in others. We can also think of mettā as the highest, most divine form of love. It is often represented by the wish "May you be happy."

We all have people and/or animals whom we love greatly. How is that kind of love different from mettā? Mettā is self-less in that there is no reference to the self in the experience. We want nothing in return; we want only for this other being to be as peaceful and easeful as possible.

In a mettā meditation practice, we can begin where a feeling of mettā arises spontaneously: perhaps when we think about babies, a favorite pet, or another being with whom we have an uncomplicated, loving relationship. Bringing mindfulness to what it feels like in the body, heart, and mind, we become familiar with the experience of mettā and bring awareness to it whenever it arises. In this way, we cultivate or expand our capacity for mettā.

Each of the brahma-viharas including mettā has a "near enemy," or a quality that resembles the immeasurable trait, but is affected by the three poisons. The near enemy of mettā is attached love, or love that is affected by craving and clinging. If we notice a strong need to be with a person or fear of losing someone, that love is affected by taṇhā. This does not mean we should write off the emotion entirely but learn to differentiate it from and transform it into mettā.

## Karuṇā (Compassion)

Karuṇā translates to compassion. It can be thought of as mettā in the presence of suffering and is sometimes felt as the quivering of the heart upon witnessing suffering. It is associated with the heart-felt wish "May you be free from suffering." Its near enemy is pity.

We know that suffering is a mark of existence in saṃsāra, and the whole of the Noble Eightfold Path is about the end of dukkha. Karuṇā is an invitation to turn *toward* the dukkha all around and within us, and to earnestly wish that we all be liberated.

Karuṇā is based in empathy in that it is choosing to try on another's perspective and witness their suffering fully, as if it were our own. In this way, karuṇā is based in wisdom: when we are aware of anattā, the division between self and others melts away so that we can see all of dukkha's pervasive manifestations. Seeing another in pain, our own heart quivers and laments the experience of dukkha, and solemnly wishes it to end.

That said, until we perfect the quality of equanimity, it is important that we practice healthy boundaries specifically with regard to empathy. Without such boundaries, we can fall into despair or experience empathy fatigue–a wearing out of our ability to feel others' experience. When this happens, the heart shuts down. To prevent this, we can cultivate equanimity alongside karuṇā, and practice empathy intentionally and with limits, gradually working to expand our capacities over time.

## Mudiṭā (Joy)

The third immeasurable heart-quality is *mudiṭā* or sympathetic joy. It can be thought of as mettā in the presence of well-being. It is

associated with the phrase "May your good fortune continue."
Its near enemy is selfish exuberance.

Like karuṇā, muditā invites us to practice empathy, but for others who are experiencing good fortune. Letting go of the division between self and other, we rejoice in the wins of those around us. Let's say a coworker is offered a promotion. An initial reaction may be one of envy (coincidentally, the far enemy of karuṇā), but we can practice muditā by imagining the joy they are experiencing and looking for a sense of closeness with the coworker, until a spark of joy appears in our own hearts. This is muditā.

We might already experience some muditā in everyday life. Perhaps when we see a dog who is absolutely ecstatic about running around the dog park or playing with a toy, we feel a sense of spontaneous joy arise in us. Whenever we notice this feeling of warmth or celebration for another, we can bring mindfulness to the experience and practice becoming familiar with muditā so that we can expand our capacity for sympathetic joy.

## Upekkhā (Equanimity)

*Upekkhā* or equanimity is sometimes considered the brahma-vihara that is the trickiest to understand. We can think of equanimity as a heart that is balanced, spacious, and nonreactive. It is associated with many phrases; one commonly used phrase is "All beings are the owners of their karma. Their happiness and unhappiness depend upon their actions, not upon my wishes for them." The near enemy of equanimity is indifference.

Equanimity refers to stability in the mind in the face of ever-changing conditions and karma. It is thus based in wisdom, specifically with regard to anicca and karma. Witnessing and empathizing with the good, neutral, or bad fortune of others and ourselves, the heart sees things clearly as they are. We see the causes of the fortune through the lens of karma, and we see that no matter our wishes for things to be a certain way, they are as they are.

In this way, equanimity carries an air of acceptance and serenity about it. It involves a letting go of trying to control anything other than our own mind and actions, allowing karma to ripen as it will. Given these aspects, equanimity also serves as a protective factor for love, compassion, and joy. Grounded in wisdom and nonreactivity, equanimity keeps us from getting carried away into the near enemies of the heart qualities.

Buddha once said that equanimity is the conditioned state that most resembles the enlightened mind. Balanced, wise, and serene, the equanimous heart offers even observation to all that we experience.

## Lessons from the Four Immeasurables

The brahma-viharas offer us the divine opportunity to melt away the artificial division between self and other and see the joy and suffering of every living being as our own. As the heart opens to its limitless loving nature, we wish wholeheartedly for the happiness of all living beings, turn toward our collective liberation from suffering, and approach our experience of samsāra with balance and wisdom.

The brahma-viharas can also serve as trainings in right concentration. As wholesome states that lead to the liberation from suffering, the brahma-viharas are recommended meditation objects for the cultivation of one-pointedness. There are a few different ways we can focus on the heart qualities in meditation. One is through their associated phrases.

After settling into the body, we can inwardly repeat a phrase associated with an immeasurable again and again for the duration of a meditation period, redirecting the mind back to the phrase each time it wanders off. We should choose a phrase that resonates with us and brings about the heart quality. We can also write our own phrases with language that organically stimulates the brahma-viharas.

## Mettā Phrases

*May you be happy*

*May you be safe from inner and outer harm*

*May you be healthy and physically well*

*May you be peaceful and at ease*

## Karunā Phrases

*May you be free from suffering*

*May you find relief and comfort*

*May you come to know true peace and ease*

## Muḍitā Phrases

*May your good fortune continue*

*May your happiness last and grow*

*May you appreciate your joy*

*I'm happy that you're happy*

## Upekkhā Phrases

*Every being owns their own karma*

*The happiness and unhappiness of others depend upon their actions, not my wishes*

*Although I care for you, I cannot keep you from suffering*

*I wish you happiness but I cannot make your choices for you*

These heart qualities also arise in everyday life and can form the basis for concentration practice. Once settled, we can call to mind the beings or situations that tend to bring about the heart quality object for us. Focusing on the person or situation, we feel into the heart. When the experience of the heart quality arises, we focus intently and concentrate on it. This is another way to cultivate wholesome one-pointedness using the brahma-viharas.

The brahma-viharas can also be directed toward the self as powerful healing tools. In formal practice, we can simply replace the "you" with "I" in the phrases, and direct the word inwardly. For an approach in daily life, we can simply turn the attention inwardly, perhaps while placing a hand on the heart, and direct the desired heart quality toward the self. When we engage in such practice, we create spaciousness around our experience that lessens cling-ing and helps us connect with our Buddha-nature. The small I or ego-self is then on the receiving end of the beautiful quality of love from the enlightened mind.

# Struggling with Self-Compassion

As Westerners, many of us struggle most with offering compassion to ourselves. We may have been conditioned to feel unworthy or not-enough. We might believe that we actually deserve the suf-fering we experience, or that we will never be free of it. Karunā invites us to explore the many opportunities to offer *ourselves* compassion throughout the day. As we heal our own hearts with the soothing balm of compassion, we grow our capacity to offer compassion to others as well.

Reflect on any regular day, beginning with waking up and ending with going to sleep. Drawing on our wisdom of dukkha and all its many forms, we will walk through the day and name as many instances of dukkha as we can observe. As we witness each instance of dukkha, we pause and feel the Heartspace. We open to the experience of suffering and ground into a commitment to mettā—to benevolence and friendliness—toward the self. With each encounter, we say to ourselves, "I see that you are suffering, and I care. May you be free from this suffering."

We might experience dukkha as soon as we hear the alarm go off. Groggy and resistant to waking up, we turn off the alarm and groan, rolling over in bed. "I see that you are suffering, and I care. May you be free from this suffering."

As we're running out the door to work, we are running late and getting stressed. Frantically looking around for keys, we spill coffee and shout an expletive. "I see that you are suffering, and I care. May you be free from this suffering."

At work we might have one or multiple uncomfortable conversations with a boss, coworker, customer, or other individual. We might feel disappointment, annoyance, frustration, or alienation. "I see that you are suffering, and I care. May you be free from this suffering."

Over our lunch break, perhaps we scarf down our food, so eager to immerse totally in the sense pleasure and wishing it would last longer than it does. "I see that you are suffering, and I care. May you be free from this suffering."

During the last hours of the work day, we stare at the clock, counting down until we can go home. Resisting being where we are, we imagine relaxing and drinking a beer when we're off. "I see that you are suffering, and I care. May you be free from this suffering."

Once off work, we sink into the couch with a drink and a snack, vegging out and allowing the mind to get lost in distraction. Although pleasurable, we forget about mindfulness and get lost in a TV show. Maybe we have one too many and fall asleep on the couch. "I see that you are suffering, and I care. May you be free from this suffering."

Perhaps this seems like an exaggerated bad day, or perhaps it seems reasonable and familiar to you. Either way, note that in any

# METTĀ MEDITATION

Find a comfortable meditation posture on a cushion, chair, lying down, or standing. Begin with a few deep, mindful breaths to help settle the body into the posture.

Once settled, place a hand over the heart. You might see if you can feel your heart beating, or simply draw attention to the Heartspace. Drawing inward, think to yourself, "May I be happy." Roll over the words in your mind until you feel a sense of warmth in the Heartspace. If you don't feel anything arise, do not worry; just stay with the phrase. "May I be happy."

After several minutes, bring to mind someone whom you love easily. Do not choose someone with whom you have a complicated relationship. A best friend or a pet work great. Imagine this being sitting with you, and think, "May you be happy." If you feel the pull to smile, let yourself do so. Repeat the phrase and feel the Heartspace. "May you be happy."

Repeat this process with a neutral acquaintance, followed by a difficult person or enemy, and ending with all living beings.

one day, we experience countless manifestations of dukkha, and all are worthy of compassion. When we direct compassion to the self in this way, we heal our sense of unworthiness and develop an unwavering commitment to liberation. May we all be free from suffering.

# EPILOGUE

———————— ✧ ————————

Together, we have learned what the Buddha taught about the nature of reality through the Three Marks of Existence and the Four Noble Truths. We have learned how to approach the path to liberation by training our bodies through moral discipline, our minds through the wisdom and concentration groups and the spiritual faculties, and hearts through the brahma-viharas. It is now up to you to determine how you will integrate these teachings into your spiritual practice and daily life.

If you are just beginning your exploration of Buddhism, I recommend you continue reading the dharma. There is a wealth of translations, interpretations, analysis, and commentary on the teachings of the Buddha from many perspectives.

I specifically encourage you to explore the three major schools of Buddhism to determine which resonates most with you. Although I have a background in both the Mahāyāna and Theravāda schools of Buddhism, this book is primarily based on the early Suttas and thus more oriented to Theravāda Buddhism. Read about Tibetan Buddhism, read about Zen, read about Vajrayāna. Let your curiosity and natural inclinations guide you.

I also recommend you seek out a sangha or spiritual community. In most major cities in the United States, you can find an Insight meditation group, a Tibetan group, a Zen center, perhaps a Shambhala center, and sometimes others. If you are not near a major city, many groups meet over Zoom. The Buddha once said that the sangha is the whole of the spiritual path. It is absolutely essential that we regularly spend time with others who are walking the Path to discuss the dharma, share practice notes, and encourage one another.

I also encourage you to seek out your own teacher. You can often find meditation teachers through Buddhist communities and retreat centers. Many teachers offer dharma talks on Dharma Seed or YouTube, and many have written books. If you want a more personal teacher-student relationship, when you find a teacher you resonate with, you can reach out to see if they are looking for students and available to meet one-on-one. Just keep in mind that in the Buddhist tradition the teachings are offered freely, and gratitude or dāna is expressed through financial support of teachers. In addition to connecting with a living teacher, I also encourage you to reflect on the life and awakening of the historical Buddha Gautama/Shakyamuni. It is important that we stay familiar with and receive guidance from those who are further along the Path than ourselves so that we can remember that awakening is possible.

By directing you to the Dharma, Sangha, and Buddha, I am asking you to go for refuge. In Buddhism, we go for refuge to the three jewels of Buddha, Dharma, and Sangha as a way of expressing our commitment to the spiritual path. Going for refuge means that when we are in need of support and guidance, we turn to the three jewels, trusting that their collective wisdom and compassion will ultimately lead to liberation. When we go for refuge to the three jewels, we express our commitment to awakening. May we all go for refuge until we collectively reach liberation, together.

# RESOURCES

There is a wealth of resources available, touching on the many aspects of Buddha's teachings, available to us. Here are select suggestions to help you deepen your learning should you choose to do so.

Dharma Seed
DharmaSeed.org
A website compilation of dharma talks given by teachers in the Vipassanā tradition.

Kim, Loundon Sumi. *Sitting Together: A Family-Centered Curriculum on Mindfulness, Meditation & Buddhist Teachings*. Somerville, MA: Wisdom Publications, 2017.
A book for children's and adult's concurrent dharma education.

*Lion's Roar*
LionsRoar.com
A self-described "mission-driven and community-supported" publication, Lion's Roar is dedicated to promoting Buddhism's "tireless wisdom" in today's world.

*Tricycle: The Buddhist Review*
Tricycle.org
An independent magazine that publishes quarterly and embraces a non-sectarian viewpoint of Buddhism.

# INDEX

## Acknowledgments

Much gratitude to my teacher, Eve Decker, for providing support, encouragement, and feedback throughout the writing process and along the Path. Many thanks to the staff of Southern Dharma Retreat Center for always being excited to discuss dharma interpretations and language. Thanks especially to Sami Walden and Anthony Pranger for providing encouragement and wisdom-consultation for engaging right action with writing. Much appreciation to Seth Varney for editing feedback, dharma discussions, and generously sharing a beautiful dharma-inspired writing space. Finally, many thanks to my kind parents for always being available and supportive to me.

## About the Author

 **Emily Griffith Burke** (she/hers/they/them) is a dharma practitioner in North Carolina. Emily lives and works as the yogi relations coordinator at Southern Dharma Retreat Center, where she supports practitioners embarking on silent meditation retreats. Emily is also a children's Sati School teacher with the Mindful Families of Durham, guest teacher with the Triangle Insight Meditation Community, and author of *Buddhism for Kids*. Emily is excited to continue practicing and living the Dharma as she embarks on graduate training in divinity and clinical mental health counseling at Wake Forest University. Find Emily at ThePracticingHuman.com.